IMPERIALISM, NATIONALISM AND REGIONALISM IN CANADIAN AND MODERN INDIAN HISTORY

Imperialism, Nationalism and Regionalism in Canadian and Modern Indian History

Edited
APARNA BASU

MANOHAR
2026

First published 1989
Reprinted 2026
First eBook edition 2026

ISBN 978-81-85054-73-5 (hardbound)
ISBN 978-93-7451-551-8 (eBook)

Published by
Ajay Kumar Jain *for*
Manohar Publishers & Distributors
4753/23 Ansari Road, Daryaganj
New Delhi 110 002

Printed and bound in India

Contents

Introduction

Canada occupies only a marginal position in the average Indian's consciousness as India does in the average Canadian's. There are certain stereotypes that haunt our imaginations, despite the migration of Indians to Canada first in the early years of the last century and later in the 1960s and Canada's more recent assistance to India in the field of engineering and technology. This exchange of men and material has obviously not produced a community of minds. For most Indians Canada is an extension of the United States, a paler version of its more dynamic southern neighbour, whereas for most Canadians India is a land of poverty, superstition, snake charmers and sadhus. These stereotypes are no doubt derived from certain objective realities obtaining in India and Canada and it would be wrong to dismiss them or play down their importance. But underneath the surface world of these misleading stereotypes are two active cultures engaged in the task of modernizing themselves without losing their distinctive identities. It is perhaps through the study of history, literature, art and other humanistic disciplines that Canada and India can hope to discover each other.

It was with this in view that it was decided that Canadian studies should be developed in a few selected universities in India. The University of Delhi was chosen as the place where study and research in Canadian history could be developed.

As a beginning in this direction an Indo-Canadian History Workshop on "Problems of Imperialism, Nationalism and Regionalism in Canadian and Modern Indian History" was organized by the University Grants Commission, the History Department of Delhi University and the Shastri Indo-Canadian Institute in December 1983. About twenty participants from different Indian universities attended the week-long seminar. In order to make the exchange between Canadian and Indian historians more meaningful, certain themes were identified where some parallels could be drawn between the Indian and the Canadian experience. Both India and Canada had been under British rule, though of course of vastly different kinds. Both are federations and the tensions between the states and the center have presented irresistible opportunities to exploit differences for partisan ends. Canada is a large, sparsely populated country of diverse provincial societies. Though these interprovincial differences are not nearly as pronounced as those between states in India, they are nevertheless real and keenly felt. Both Canada and India are plural societies and both have had regional movements based on ethnic, linguistic and religious differences. Canada and India have had some common experiences in the course of their economic development also. Regional imbalances and unequal economic growth have generated a lot of discontent in both countries.

The Canadian historians presented an overview of different aspects of Canadian history, and rightly so, since they were addressing an audience by and large unfamiliar with Canadian history. The Indian papers, on the other hand, had a narrower focus and were based on primary sources and research donc by the scholars themselves.

Prof. Cornelius Jaenen has done extensive work in the field of French relations with Canada's native peoples. His prize winning *Friend and Foe: Aspects of French Amerindian Cultural Contact* is a seminal work in this area. It is commonly believed that the French contact experience with the Amerindians was unique. Francis Parkman, in the late nineteenth century, wrote: "Spanish civilisation crushed the Indian, English civilisation scorned and ignored him; French civilisation embraced and cherished him." This belief was canonized in France in the *genie colonial* thesis, the assertion that the French possessed a peculiar ability and facility for getting along with the native peoples. In view of this, France seemed destined to assume a *mission civilsatrice* abroad. Professor Jaenen questions this accepted view of the superiority of the French in dealing with aboriginal people and feels that it needs to be qualified in many respects. There was no single French view of the natives, no one intellectual construct that dominated the field. There were a wide range of views ranging from those held by men like Rabelais or Montaigne who romanticised the Indians as men in the state of nature, unspoilt and untainted to those like Cornelius de Pauw who regarded them as idiot children, incapable of mental progress. According to Jaenen, the uniqueness of French relations with the Amerindians lay not in that it was more benevolent or superior to other but that it was characterised by a consistent, unitary and centralised policy. The French also exploited the Continent without occupation. The French experience with aboriginal rights and titles as well as the French system of reserves was also unique. This experience played a role in the emergence of a theoretical framework for the social sciences concerned with native peoples, the 'mode of production' concept.

In his paper on the "Evolution of Nationalism in French Canada", Prof. Ramsay Cook, whose *Maple Leaf Forever* is a standard book on nationalism in Canada, highlights some of the paradoxes in contemporary Canada. One of the paradoxes of the very recent years was that of Pierre Trudeau and Rene Levesque, both Qubecers, but the former an uncompromising champion of Canadian federalism, the latter an equally strong supporter of a sovereign Quebec. Trudeau's policies, the Official Language Act, promoting the use of French in public service, his energy policy, were all designed to meet Quebec's needs. While Quebecers voted for Trudeau's Liberal Party at the Centre, Levesque's *parti quebecois* won an overwhelming victory in the provincial elections. In Ottawa, Trudeau's liberals were committed to a constitution that made French and English equal languages. In Quebec city *parti quebecois* equally firmly supported by Quebec voters continued to promote an unilingually French-speaking society. As Professor Cook rightly points out Levesque's nationalism is an extremely cautious one, bearing little or no similarity to nationalist movements in the Third World.

Cook attempts to explain this apparent paradox in the light of Quebec's history. The memory of conquest, fear of extinction because of defeat is a central part of French Canadian experience. Throughout their history, French Canadians have been preoccupied with their minority position. One can draw some parallels between this and the Muslim fears in India of being a minority community, though of course there are many differences including the demographical. The French in Canada are concentrated in one province while the Muslims in India were unevenly distributed in various parts of the country. Fear of the future and hope for the future combine to create indecision, ambiguity and paradox. Duality of allegiance whereby French Canadians elect different parties at the centre and in the province, according to Cook, testifies to the political sagacity of the French Canadians.

Canada consists of five distinct regions – the Maritimes, Quebec,

Ontario, the Prairie West and British Columbia. The Prairie West has not only been one of the most clearly demarcated regional entities but it has been the most restless and impatient. The main feature of the region is its geographical isolation from the rest of Canada. The Prairie West was the creation of the federal government. From the formal purchase of the territory in 1870 until 1930, the federal government administered and developed the area. Prof. Carl Berger shows how the West was developed as a wheat granary. Prairie society and its regional character was shaped in the formative period by the immigration policies of the federal government. By 1914 each of the Prairie provinces contained substantial minorities of non-British origin. Prairie society became ethnically diverse and a high proportion of its people had no experience of Canada and no sentimental attachments to its political or other institutions. One factor which nurtured a regional sentiment and led to the growth of the Progressive party in the 1920s was the exploitation of the West by the East.

The Co-operative Commonwealth Federation and the Social Credit Movement were also expressions of the regional sentiment. The tradition of a third party protest inaugurated by the Progressives and sustained by C.C.F. and Social Credit Movement became one of the distinctive features of the political culture of Prairie West. But this did not mean repudiation of national parties or rejection of Canada. Neither of the three parties were separatist. Till the end of World War II the Prairie West could be termed a region. But the basis of regionalism gradually altered, as people turned to non-agricultural occupations. With the development of new resources and urbanization, westerners have become in social character and outlook like other Canadians. Agrarian grievance and regional identity have begun to disappear. Hostility to Liberal policies and pro-Conservative sentiments are now expressed through national not regional parties. Berger points out quite rightly and Indian historians will whole-heartedly agree with him that regional sentiment is not only reflected by politicians, it is partly created by them. Prairie regionalism arose out of the geographical isolation of the area from the rest of Canada, the fact that it was an exclusively agrarian economy and the subordinate relation of that economy to the industrial east. Despite a series of unsuccessful revolts against the central authority, there are strong ties of culture and sentiment that link the west to the rest of Canada.

Professor Nelles, an economic historian of eminence, in his paper on "Interpreting Canadian Economic Development" gives an extremely lucid and comprehensive overview of the historiography of Canadian economic development. Canada is a rich, highly industrialised country. With less than 0.5 per cent of the world's population, it produces 4 per cent of the world's total exports. Its gross national product of 253 billion dollars in 1980 ranked it seventh among the OECD countries. Over the last century Canadian output has grown in real terms at an average rate of 40 per cent per decade, population by 19 per cant and real domestic product per capita by 18 per cent. Nevertheless, this quantitatively impressive history of Canadian economic development has always been clouded by a fundamental doubt. Concerning Canada's growth and relative wealth, there is no question. Opinion is, however, sharply divided over the course of this development. Is Canada an example of a normal industrial economy evolving towards maturity and industrialisation, or is it a case of distorted, dependent development? This question has divided scholars who laid down the first analytical framework for the study of Canadian economic history and continues to perplex economic historians even today.

Professor Nelles begins with the first and most enduring interpretation of Canadian economic development – the Staples Theory – put forward simultaneously but separately by W.A. Mackintosh and H.A. Innes in the 1920s and 1930s. According to this, Canada developed on the strength of a succession of staple trades – cod fish, beaver pelts, timber, wheat, non-ferrous metals, pulp and paper. Though the staple might change, certain broad features remained the same – external dependence on markets, capital, and technology. The staple approach was enshrined in the next generation by W.T. Easterbrook and H.G.J. Aitken in their influential textbook, *Canadian Economic History* (1956).

The staples theory was challenged by economic historians using quantitative techniques in the late 1950s and 1960s, but Kenneth Buckley, Chamber, Gordon and others did not, however, provide any alternative analytical framework.

Professor Nelles also deals with the Marxist and Neo-Marxist or Neo-nationalist interpretations such as that of Kari Levitt in "Silent Surrender" where she argues that Canada has been drawn into a new kind of dependence on foreign capital.

Nelles holds that some of these tracts were written more for use in an ongoing political struggle than as historical analysis.

The different interpretations outlined in this paper show the hybrid nature of Canadian economic development. Canada falls within the broad pattern of western industrialisation but it has a strong tinge of dependence to provide links with the economic regions on the margins of industrialisation. Hence Canadian economic history is not entirely irrelevant for Indian scholars.

The "deindustrialisation" debate has been of considerable importance in Indian economic history. There are broadly three main schools of thought on this subject. The nationalist and Marxist scholars argue that British rule destroyed Indian handicrafts. Deindustrialisation was a metaphor of colonial exploitation. This was the view put forward by R.C. Dutt, Shelvankar, Pandit Madan Mohan Malaviya, Gandhiji and in a more sophisticated manner by Prof. Amiya Bagchi in more recent years. Their arguments are based on import-export trade figures, output and employment statistics and contemporary descriptive evidence. In the 1950s this view was challenged by Daniel Thorner on the basis of some qualitative evidence; mainly population data based on Census Reports. Thorner found no decline between 1881 and 1931 in the number of people employed in the handicrafts-handloom sector. A third view was put forward by Morris D. Morris who tried to show that there was no deindustrialisation.

Dr. J. Krishnamurti's paper has to be viewed in the light of these three paradigms. He examines the broad trends in India's premier handicraft, the cotton handloom industry, considering loomage, employment and output for the period 1800-1900 and 1900-1940. He concludes that there was decline but in different regions at different times, and periods of decline may be followed by upward trends. For India as a whole, it could be safely said that handloom output declined over the nineteenth century. Even for the period 1900-1950, the expansion in the twentieth century probably did not make up for the sharp decline that had already taken place.

Prof. P.S. Gupta using some new material from the cabinet papers shows how in the period after 1917, the imperial power was more vulnerable than before and to maintain authority, constitutional adjustments had to be made along with a reshuffling of priorities. Among these were administrative devolution, provincial autonomy and the federation of component units. These devices were used by the colonial government to deflect all-India challenges to British rule. "Provincial Autonomy", liberal as it was, smacked of divide and rule. The paper deals with the years 1927-1939 and analyses two of the contradictions within colonial interest that were revealed in some detail, the problem of transferring the law and order portfolio and the distribution of the income tax between the centre and the provinces.

Prof. Aparna Basu's paper, in a way complements Prof. Ramsay Cook's and Prof. Carl Berger's papers on sub-nationalism and regionalism in Canada. While bilingualism, denominational schools, quotas and reservations were devices for promoting national unity in Canada, in India they encouraged divisiveness and promoted separatism. Unlike Canada, in India, religious and linguistic differences did not coincide.

Professor Basu's paper concentrates on Hindu and Muslim communalism in India in the pre-Independence period and particularly on how education contributed to the growth of communal consciousness. The paper examines in some detail government education policy as well as the growth of denominational institutions like the Muhammedan Oriental College, Aligarh University, Benares Hindu University and the proliferation of Maktabs and Madrasas. The impact of education on communal polities and *vice versa* is discussed with special reference to Bengal, a Muslim majority province where Muslims were educationally backward and the United Provinces, a Hindu majority province where Muslims were educationally advanced. As Professor Berger points out Prairie regionalism was never separatist in intention and as Professor Cook shows even in Quebec the majority do not want political independence. The regional problem was not felt with the same degree of intensity in Canada as in India. The Muslim League, on the other hand, after 1940 demanded a separate homeland and the movement finally ended in the partition of the subcontinent. This volume is published with the hope that it will stimulate further comparative studies in Indian and Canadian History.

1

THE UNIQUENESS OF THE FRENCH RELATIONSHIP WITH CANADA'S NATIVE PEOPLES, 1504-1763

Cornelius J. Jaenen

I

The French experience with the native peoples of New France, collectively known as Amerindians,* seems to have been unique in the annals of colonial history. Their relationship appears to have been singular, uncommon and in some respects the only one of its kind when considered in a comparative framework. In other words, the French contact experience in North America differed from the Anglo-American, or the later British, or even the subsequent British Canadian relationship with Amerindian peoples.

This thesis is well-established in our historiography and therefore, on the face of it, one should have little new to say about early race and culture contact relations. More penetrating and critical examination of the circumstances of interaction, however, reveals hitherto unsuspected aspects of the relationship which evolved between the French and Amerindian bands and tribes. Indeed, the accepted view of French superiority in dealing with aboriginal peoples needs to be qualified in many respects and its ideological basis seriously questioned, if not rejected outrightly. On the other hand, the unique bonds established between the French and Amerindians also deserve to be better known.

---

*I employ the term Amerindian, an unambiguous and practical appelation, in the same sense as one uses European or African—i.e., to refer to peoples of many different cultures, languages and traditions who historically share a continent and can be perceived by "outsiders" as sharing certain broad social, political and intellectual attributes. Indian as a Columbian misnomer which requires some qualification such as West, East, American of Canadian.

The belief that the French relationship was unique, or notably different from the Anglo-American approach, was well-established in French, British and even Amerindian minds during the colonial period. In France this conviction eventually was canonized in the *génie colonial* thesis, the assertion that the French possessed a peculiar ability and facility for getting along with native peoples, a national trait of compatibility. In view of this supposedly inherent Gallic quality, France seemed destined to assume a *mission civilisatrice* abroad. This interpretation also stressed the negative qualities of Iberian and Britannic colonisation, for in the 18th century the French had rediscovered Las Casas and his indictment of the conquistadores, and had revived their 16th century Black Legend charging the Spaniards with genocide, the systematic extermination of 15 to 20 million people. Even Voltaire recalled first-hand description of Amerindians hunted down by fierce dogs and of natives hanged publicly in groups of thirteen. These nationalistic views, stressing the benign French approach to native peoples, were propagated by writers as diverse in background as the naturalist Buffon, the polemicist de Pauw, and the soldier Duret.[1]

In North America, Governor Vaudreuil opined that the southern tribes "prefer the French to all other nations." The missionary Charlevoix, who wrote a six volume history of the colony in the 1740s, added that his nation was "the only one which has had the secret of winning the affection of the American natives." The trader Jérémie, who intruded into the regions claimed by the Hudson's Bay Company, found that the northern hunting bands received the French as "brothers" but, said he, "they do not have the same attachment for the English." He was restating an affirmation made a generation earlier in Louisiana, where an officer remarked that although the English of Carolina "appear richer and more liberal to them, yet they do not find their intercourse as pleasant as that of the French."[2]

These sentiments were confirmed when Canada fell into British hands. Mme. de Pompadour confided to a correspondent:

> It seems they will have much difficulty establishing themselves well in Canada; the natives still like the French and do all the harm they can to their new masters. I do not believe that there is any nation which possesses so well the art of making itself hated as the English. . . .[3]

Brissot the Warville in his travels found the same sentiments after the American Revolution. He observed:

> A touching fact, which will give us a good idea of the virtues and of the gratitude of these people, is the affection they retain for the French. A man of that nation can travel in safety, unarmed, from Canada to the Illinois. The natives distinguish by his manners, his skin, his language, to which nation he belongs and they entertain him like a brother. But if he is found in the company of Americans, they treat him with the same cruelty, for they detest the Americans.[4]

These sentiments confirm the sentiments of the native prophet who aroused Pontiac's supporters against the Anglo-Americans in 1763, "these dogs dressed in red, who have come to rob you of your hunting grounds, and drive away the game." The Great Lakes tribes were asked to "take up the hatchet" against them, to "wipe them from the face of the earth," adding that "the children of your great father, the King of France, are not like the English," that they "love the red men," and even the improbable "they understand the true mode of worshipping me" which referred to a revitalization movement. Or, again, the Saulteaux chief who told the trader Alexander Henry in the autumn of 1761 that he knew "our father, the King of France, is old and infirm" and tired of making war so he had fallen asleep and consequently Canada had been conquered. But, he warned, "this slumber is drawing to a close. Already I hear our father waking up and asking about the fate of his children, the Indians."[5]

English commentaries at the time do not seem to have been in disagreement with these views. An observer in 1755 conceded that "the French have always had a great advantage over the English in treating with them." An anonymous pamphleteer specified that "according to their superior dexterity in address and civility of usage, they are more successful than we, in procuring and retaining their friendship." The clearest statement remains Thomas Mante's judgment in his *History of the Late War in North America*:

> . . . and it must be owned, that the general behaviour of the French to the Indians was so very different from that of the English, as to give all the weight the French could wish to those

> lessons; the effects of which, accordingly, became every day more and more visible. We mention these particulars, not only to recommend the manner in which the French treat the Indians as highly deserving to be imitated by us; but to wear out of the minds of our deluded countrymen as are not entirely destitute of good sense and humanity, the prejudice conceived against an innocent, much abused, and once happy people, who, with all their simplicity, are no strangers to the first principles of morality; and, accordingly, entertain as deep a sense of the justice, benevolence, and condescension of their former friends, the French, as they do of the injustice, cruelty, and insolence, with which they have been used by their present fellow-subjects, the English.[6]

His appraisal attributed the French colonizing genius to an espousal of the myth of the *bon sauvage*, the Noble Savage of primitivist and romantic literature, but also to an absence of the racism which marked the Anglo-Saxon contact.

The school of French imperial historians gave it great prominence after 1870. Georges Hardy wrote that his countrymen "have been delivered more quickly of primitive expansionism and we have from the beginning incorporated with our needs of colonial domination the scruples of civilized peoples and the concern of educators." André Julien added that the "French had without argument a gift for conciliating the aborigines that no other people possessed to the same degree." Hubert Deschamps, in describing French colonial doctrines since the 16th century, states that "their gift of sympathy (for the Amerindians), their facility of assimilation, their absence of racism were there from the beginning."[7]

The English-speaking world since Edmund Burke has generally adopted the same interpretation. No historian expressed the thesis more elegantly and succinctly than did the "Boston brahmin" Francis Parkman in the late 19th century: "Spanish civilization crushed the Indian; English civilization scorned and neglected him; French civilization embraced and cherished him." Philip Means, writing in 1965, commended the "singularly sympathetic and conciliating spirit which Frenchmen have always displayed toward races distinct from their own." Mason Wade affirmed as dean of Canadian studies in the United States that the French exemplified "a peculiar ability to conciliate aboriginal people" and win their confidence.[8]

These are some of the elements of the ideological background of our topic.

II

Was this presumably felicitous relationship accompanied by positive, optimistic and constructive assessments of native character and culture? Very early in the French contact experience a wide range of views emerged, among them contradictory evaluations even within the writings of a single author. Writers throughout Western Europe, including the few who had first-hand experience in the New World, portrayed Amerindians according to the traditional philosophical concepts and intellectual constructs that were part of their cultural baggage and bias. There were optimistic assessments couched in the frameworks of the Golden Age, the Earthly Paradise, the Millennial Kingdom, the Lost Tribes of Israel, and Christian Utopianism; but, there were also pessimistic assessments couched in the frameworks of the Chain of Being, the Monstruous World, Wild Men, and Satanic domination. The emergence of positive themes such as the Noble Savage myth, the Four Stages theory, inevitable progress and human perfectibility requires balancing with the emergence of negative themes such as colonial degeneration, the Vanishing Red Man thesis, figurism, and the infancy of the New World. Not infrequently Spanish views of contact in Central and South America were simply adopted by the French as sufficient explanation and rationalization of their own developing experience in the northern hemisphere. The Spanish assessment was much more complex and controversial than is widely suspected, so the French inherited, for example, the contradictory views expressed in the acrimonious confrontation known as the Great Debate of Valladolid in 1550-51.[9]

The Renaissance writers, Rabelais, Ronsard and Montaigne, on the basis of travellers' tales, the gossip of fishermen in the port taverns, and glimpses of occasional exotically bedecked Amerindian captives exhibited on public and religious occasions, set the pattern for an optimistic and romantic interpretation which passed into literature and history as the myth of the noble savage. Montaigne wrote:

> Those people are wild, just as we call wild the fruits that Nature has produced by herself and in her normal course; whereas really

> it is those that we have changed artificially and led astray from the common order that we should rather call wild.[10]

Montaigne initiated not only the concept of the natural man, unspoiled by social artificiality, but also indicated an effective and safe method of employing the New World and its cultures to criticize both church and state, both European man and European institutions.

Of equal antiquity and tenacity was the view of the Amerindian as a cruel, ferocious sub-human, treacherous brute, and cannibalistic savage. The savagery/civility dichotomy, which became implicit in so much of anthropological and historical writing, was explicitly and unashamedly present in many French assessments from the foundations of New France. In 1558 André Thévet described Amerindians as "a marvellously strange, wild and brutish people, without faith, without law, without religion and without any civilities, but living like unreasoning beasts as nature has produced them, eating roots, men as well as women remaining ever naked, until perhaps such time as they will be frequented by Christians, from whom they will little by little learn to put off this brutishness to put on more civil and human ways."[11] Savagery was defined as absence of certain qualities and institutions. *Sauvages* were people devoid of civility, those possessing *ni foi, ni roi, ni loi*, as the popular expression phrased it. They were often seen as bestial men, *homines sylvestris*, or the wild, hairy, naked, lustful and dangerous beings who lived beyond the pale of organized life in the forests, fulfilling their animalistic instincts, while largely ignorant of God and morality. Jacques Cartier described them as "savage peoples living without a knowledge of God and the use of reason," and later Samuel de Champlain wrote of hostile tribes as "brute beasts having neither faith nor law, living without God and religion."[12]

Towards the end of the French régime, during the Age of the Enlightenment, the stereotype persisted. The great naturalist, the Comte de Buffon, gave the scientific assessment of America's native peoples as barely human because still sunken in *animalité*, subject to most natural phenomena, passive beings, almost inert peoples in static cultures in terms of dominating their environment. In his *Epoques de la Nature*, he generalized from the northern nomadic hunting bands for all Amerindians:

> . . . having never brought into submission either the animals or the elements, having neither conquered the seas nor directed the course of rivers, nor cultivated the soil, he was in himself only an animal of the first order, and existed merely as a being of little consequence, a kind of powerless automation incapable of reforming or reinforcing nature.[13]

The debate continued whether the Amerindians were people in the infancy of mankind or degenerated populations. Buffon, in his *Histoire naturelle* (1749), supposed they were of post-Adamite origin because of their lack of material and cultural development. He tried to situate them in the context of "the general contraction of animated Nature throughout the whole Continent." He explained:

> In the savage, the organs of generation are small and feeble. He has no hair, no beard, no ardour for the female. Though nimbler than the European, because more accustomed to running, his strength is not so great. His sensations are less acute; and yet he is more cowardly and timid. He has no vivacity, no activity of mind. . . .[14]

.lthough Buffon believed, as did most of his contemporaries, that human nature was everywhere the same, he related racial or national differences to such factors as climate and environment, and consequently, to his consternation, he was cited as an authority on colonial degeneration.

The theory of colonial degeneration received its clearest, most virulent and doctrinaire expression in the writings of Cornelius de Pauw. He argued that plants, animals, men, and possibly institutions, inevitably degenerated in the unfavorable American environment. Only snakes, insects and harmful animals prospered. Amerindians were its natural men; consequently, they were idiot children, incurably lazy, and incapable of any mental progress. De Pauw argued that physical degeneration was accompanied by moral and intellectual decline:

> . . . degeneration had attacked their senses and their organs; their soul had lost proportionately to the decline of their body. Nature having taken everything from one hemisphere of this globe in order to give it to the other, had placed in America only children,

> of whom it as yet had been unable to make men. When Europeans first reached the West Indies, in the fifteenth century, there was not a single American who could read or write: in our day there is still no American who can think.[15]

He undermined his own thesis somewhat through exaggeration–for even the most gullible French readers found it difficult to believe some Amerindians had pyramidal or conical craniums, and that many animals lost their tails and dogs their bark in America.

The *abbé* Raynal combined the degeneracy thesis with the figurist views of many of the Jesuit missionaries at the time to arrive at his own interpretation. He relied heavily on the testimony of the missionary Joseph François Lafitau who saw the religion of the Iroquois among whom he labored as an imperfect survival of an earlier universal revelation which God had given to primitive peoples and which was the foundation of a universal cultural unity. He wrote:

> Everything points to some sickness from which the human race still suffers. The ruin of this world is still imprinted on the faces of its inhabitants; a race of men degraded and degenerated in their physical constitution, in their build, in their way of life, and in their minds which show so little aptitude for all the arts of civilization. . . .[16]

However, Raynal mixed his images and his logic became uncertain at times: he depicted Amerindians as decrepit and deteriorating, like the universe, and then suddenly he depicted them as immature and in the infancy of mankind. He had also written:

> The indifference of the males towards the other sex to which Nature has entrusted the place of reproduction suggests an organic imperfection, a sort of infancy of the people of America similar to that of the individuals of our continent who have not yet reached the age of puberty. It is a deeprooted failing of that other hemisphere, a sort of impotence that reveals clearly how new the continent is. . . .[17]

It was on the basis of such views that the religious in New France had concluded that the native peoples required tutors and executors because they were incapable of administering their own affairs.

The existence of 18th century philosophical pessimism has often been obscured by the emphasis placed upon Enlightenment perfectibility, progress, cosmopolitanism and rationalism. No single intellectual construct dominated the field and none was able to encompass the great diversity of views or to reflect the spectrum of interpretations. The discovery of America and the contact with "new men", according to some *philosphes*, may not only have been the most important event in European history but also the most disastrous event

III

The French relationship with the Amerindians may have been unique in the measure that it was characterized by a consistent, unitary and centralized policy. It has sometimes been argued that New France was subject to arbitrary and despotic government, stifling metropolitan mercantilist economic controls, and burdensome clerical and seigneurial interference with personal liberty and innovation. On the other hand, it can be demonstrated that the colonial government which functioned through correspondence with the Ministry of the Marine, was more paternalistic than despotic. There was sensitivity to colonial and Amerindian interests as bureaucrats proceeded through consultations with local notables who were sensitive to commercial and military issues. It can be argued that traditional hierarchical society transplanted in the colony provided stability and order.

Perhaps what we indicate as being a particular strength of the French relationship with the Amerindians is merely the reverse of the Anglo-American ineffectiveness and chaotic disunity and inconsistency in dealing with the native peoples. Each British colony had its own particular policy, seldom in agreement with that of its neighbours, often at odds with trading partnerships, legislative assemblies and land speculators, nearly always in disagreement with Imperial policies. Even after the defeat of Dieskau in 1755, Thomas Mante acknowledged the superiority of the French relationship:

> These troops, with the Canadians, who were as well, if not better qualified for service in that country, than the French regulars, joined to the numerous tribes of Indians in the French interest, being conducted by one chief, formed as infinitely more for-

> midable power that the regular and provincial troops of the English, who could not unite their strength on account of the jarring interests of the different provinces.[18]

Amerindian affairs were within the jurisdiction of the Governor-General in New France, who was also the chief military officer and the King's representative. Onontio (as he was called) spoke with authority, often commanded respect from friendly and unfriendly tribes alike, was careful to observe the protocol and even vocabulary associated with gift exchanges, formalization of alliances, distribution of prisoners and booty; he represented a line of conduct applicable from Micmac and Abenakis country in the east to the Sioux and Cree country in the west. Generally, the tribes knew where they stood in their trade and warfare arrangements, and when there were shifts in French tactics and local practice, Canadian officers who commanded at the scattered posts were instructed to explain how long-term strategy and alliances remained unchanged.[19] Missionaries were often influential in maintaining the "allied tribes" faithful to the French cause. Indeed, missionaries such as the *abbé* Maillard, the *abbé* Le Loutre and Father Rasle were far less certain of their own influence upon the Micmacs and Abenakis than were their English enemies.

An important aspect of the consistent French policy was the avoidance of authoritarian overbearing and of pretension to rule the tribes of the upper country. A perceptive British observer reported in 1755 on the "secret", as he called it, of French influence among the Amerindians in comparison to British lack of success:

> They know too well the Spirit of the Indian Politicks to affect a Superiority of Government over the Indians; Yet they have in Reality & Truth, of more solid Effect an Influence an Ascendency in all the Councils of all the Indians on the Continent and lead and direct their Measures, Not even Our Own Allies the Six Nations excepted.[20]

Just as Versailles through its officials in the colony was sensitized to the limitations on the exercise of its authority and to the Canadian love of liberty, so the officials at Quebec, through the network of posts and mission stations manned by Marine soldiers, *congé* holders and missionaries, were sensitized to the needs of the native peoples and the limitations on the exercise of French sovereignty.

IV

Another unique characteristic of the French contact was the exploitation of the continent without the occupation at the same time of that vast expanse. Unlike the situation in the Anglo-American colonies, there was no westward moving frontier of white settlement necessitating dispossession of the native peoples. New France was a collection of small seaboard settlements–Acadia, Isle Royale and Louisiana–and the valley of the St. Lawrence, which had been inhabited when first visited by Cartier and settled briefly by Roberval in the 16th century but which had become a no-man's-land by the time Champlain founded his *habitation* at Quebec in 1608 and the religious zealots founded Ville-Marie (Montreal) in 1642. There were posts in the interior with a small nucleus of French soldiers, farmers and traders–at Detroit, Michilimackinals, and Kaskaskia, for example. The matters of discussion with the native inhabitants, among whom the French lived more as guests than as rulers, revolved round fur trade issues, inter-tribal wars, the brandy traffic, and missionary activities and not, as in the case of the English, round land cession, settlement and treatment of captives. The missionary *abbé* Gaulin expressed it clearly: "the natives are of little account, when our allies, but could become of considerable importance were they our enemies."[21]

In our recent historiography, it has become fashionable to portray the Amerindians as victims of European exploitation and as pawns in Imperials rivalries and wars. This is a depiction which does little justice to Amerindian independence, initiative and ability to exploit European involvement in the continent to native advantages. The French were unique perhaps in the sense that their experience in the hinterland, or upper Canada, quickly taught them that they were obliged in matters both of war and of trade to keep in mind constantly the Amerindian interests. Le Maire's memorandum of 1717 defined the situation succinctly:

> The Trade with the Indians is a necessary commerce; and even if the colonists were able to manage without it, the State is virtually forced to maintain it, if it wishes to maintain Peace, unless one wished to follow the cruel resolution of destroying all the Indians,

> which is contrary at once to both nature and Religion. There is no middle course; one must have the natives either as friend or foe; and whoever wants him as a friend, must furnish him with his necessities at conditions which allow him to procure them.[22]

The Intendant Raudot said that it was impossible to force French military or commercial policy on them: "We can only solicit them not to deal with the English and we can in no way prevent them from doing so." One English observer, in commenting on the alleged failure of French officers to prevent atrocities being committed on English prisoners by Amerindian warriors, stressed the limitations of French authority and jurisdiction over their allies:

> Moreover, the balance of power of North-America, was now in the hands of the savages; and however humanity might urge M. de Montcalm to interfere with his whole force, reasons of policy and duty to his country bade him not hazard the consequences that might attend such a step.[23]

There was no question of coercion or threat in dealing with native peoples.

Nevertheless, it is true that Amerindians became increasingly dependent on European trade goods and services. Similarily, Frenchmen became dependent on Amerindian hospitality, support and services. Neither party was able to extricate itself from this relationship, although there is documentary evidence to indicate that there were times when each party would have welcomed such a possible course of action. A memorandum prepared for the Ministry of the Marine in 1730 reminded French bureaucrats of this North American reality:

> It is agreed and it is a fact that generally all the natives like and fear the French, mistrust the English and believe all our goods to be superior; and they recognize that they cannot get along without our powder, without our white blankets, our cloth for over-clothing, our vermillion, cutlery, trinkets–so there are only yard-goods and kettles which they obtain more reasonably from the English and which are two items to which our attention must be turned. . . .[24]

The assertion made by Innis, and repeated in most general histories, to the effect that English trade goods were of superior quality and more cheaply priced than French trade goods, seems questionable. It may have been true of the French hemmed in on Isle Royale. But it was not so, for example, in the Hudson's Bay region. One Hudson Bay Company factor wrote (1728):

> Never was any man so upbraided with our powder, kettles and hatchets, than we have been this summer by all the natives, especially by those that borders near the French.[25]

This was by no means an isolated comment in the Honorable London company's correspondence.

V

The French experience with aboriginal rights or title, if not entirely unique, was at least difficult from the Anglo-American approach. Property was conceived by Europeans as being the basis of the social order; yet, during the Enlightenment, some theorists attacked its accumulation through inheritance and rank and regarded it as the basis for inequities. The *abbé* Pierre Dolivier, for example, went so far as to assert that "the earth belongs to all in common, and to no one in particular," while Morelly in *Codes de la Nature* (1755) ranked in first place the precept that "nothing shall belong to anyone individually as his sole property, except such things as he puts to his personal use, whether for his needs, his pleasure, or his daily work."[26] These were views most Amerindians would have supported. They saw land as being no more the absolute possession of any individual than the air one breathed!

That is not to say that Amerindians had no concept of possessory rights. The English traders had to obtain Iroquois permission to cross their territories to the Western tribes. The Montagnais granted right of passage across band territory, sometimes exacting a toll, in what anthropologists have called the hunting range system. The Montagnais were fearful that this right might not be respected when the five Postes du Roi passed to the British in 1760, and they instructed their missionary to appeal to the commander of the British occupation forces:

> Our father, we learn that our lands are to be given away not only to trade thereon but also to give them in full title to various individuals. . . . We have always been a free nation, and now we will become slaves, which would be very difficult to accept after having enjoyed our liberty for so long.[27]

The implication in this statement is that, under French rule, even in the territory around Tadoussac which had been reserved as the Postes du Roi and closed to colonization, the native peoples were free and independent.

The French views were never explicitly enunciated because it was not necessary to do so. They quickly came to view the Amerindians as first immigrants, not autochthonous peoples, probably of Asiatic origin. The St. Lawrence valley was unoccupied territory open to colonization according to prevalent "law of nature" concepts. The French claim to occupancy, therefore, was similar to the Amerindian claim to occupancy–that is, on grounds of *vacuum domicilium.*[28] Some jurists, among them the renowned Emmerich de Vattel, still chose to believe that Amerindians did not take possession of their lands in the sense of cultivating and exploiting them: "The peoples of those vasts tracts of land rather roamed over them than inhabited them".[29] Prior discovery became the primary basis of European claim to legitimate ownership in the 18th century as transfers of sovereignty and title were made.

In New France there was no alienation of Amerindian lands, and little vacation of lands. Governor Courcelles said in 1665 that the King's will was that "all adult subjects treat the Indians with kindness, justice and equity, never resorting to violence against them, nor will anyone take the lands on which they are living under the pretext that it would be better and more suitable if they were French."[30] There was no displacement of native populations to make way for white European settlement; there was no advancing and threatening frontier of colonization. Instead, there were native peoples settled within the French seigneurial tract in the St. Lawrence valley on *réserves* administered by the missionary clergy, and there were also small islands of French settlement scattered at strategic commercial and military locations in the Amerindian hinterlands. The French, like other European powers, claimed sovereignty over the lands they "discovered" and employed symbolic acts such as planting crosses, nailing the King's coat of arms on trees, or burying inscribed lead plates to establish this claim against the claims of European rivals. La Vérendrye's son took possession of the lands west of the Mandans in March 1743 by secretly burying a lead plate, and then erected a stone cairn, saying to the local inhabitants that he was doing so "in memory of our coming to their lands."[31]

It would seem that under French sovereignty, Amerindian nations were regarded as independent and free, so long as they maintained friendly trade and military relations, and they were willing to receive missionaries. They were *nations* because conceived of as an ethnic group specific to a particular geographical location: they were not *états* because they were not believed to be organized under sovereign governments possessing coercive powers, and therefore they were not among the diplomatically recognized "family of nations". Voltaire attacked the prevalent concept with his usual cynicism and vigour:

> The so-called savages of America are sovereign peoples who receive ambassadors from our colonies transplanted in their territories through greed and frivolity. They know honour which our savages of Europe have never heard spoken about. They have a mother country, they love her, they defend her . . . they fight with courage and often speak with heroic forcefulness.[32]

The missionary Charlevoix said that although they made war like barbarians "it must however be allowed that in treaties of peace, and generally in all negotiations, they display such dexterity, address and elevation of soul, as would to honour to the most civilized nations." Although they looked upon themselves "as the lords and sovereigns of the soil," they were "not so jealous of their property as to find fault with newcomers who settle on it, provided they do not attempt to molest them."[33] Hospitality and peaceful co-existence seemed to characterize the relationship, so long as dominance, coercion and authoritarianism were avoided by the French.

The case of the Iroquois is an especially illuminating one because after 1713, by the terms of the Treaty of Utrecht, they theoretically came under British sovereignty. The French claimed they had made a formal submission to them in 1666, a fact reaffirmed by numerous *prises de possession*, but all the Five Nations themselves would concede was that they had extended hospitality and had promised that the French "would always be assured of a lodge among them" and that the missionary "would always find his mat to welcome him."[34] A memorandum on missions in 1712 stated:

> It must seem that the Iroquois recognize no masters. And although the French have posted the coat of arms of France among them before and after the English posted those of England, they nevertheless recognize no domination. That is what they reiterated and tried to establish twice during two assemblies which they held in Montreal during the summer of the present year. To leave in perpetuity marks of their independence from both the English and the French, they had an act drawn up in proper form to which they put their signs and native hieroglyphs.[35]

The French exploited such sentiments against the British. The Ministry of Marine expressed great satisfaction with La Galissonnière's tactics in this respect: "These Indians claim to be and in effect are independent of all nations, and their lands incontestably belong to them." A military report on the boundaries of the colony, dated 1755, expressed the official French view:

> The Savages in question are free and independent and there are none who may be termed subjects of one crown or the other. The declaration of the Treaty of Utrecht in this respect is erroneous and cannot alter the nature of things. . . . These savage nations are governed only by themselves. . . .[36]

The Micmacs were quite emphatic in their assertions to the French Governor at Louisbourg when they challenged France's right to cede their lands to Britain:

> But learn from us that we are on this ground which you trod under food and upon which you walk as the trees which you see have started to come forth from it. It is ours and nothing will ever be able to take it away from us or make us abandon it.[37]

Governor St. Ovide replied that he knew well that "the lands on which I tread, you possess them from all time," and then added that "the King of France your Father never had the intention of taking them from you" but had ceded only his own rights to the British crown. This was a fine distinction between French sovereignty and Amerindian possession and rights of usufruct. At best, the French claim was what the Intendant Claude Thomas Dupuy termed joint ownership or "sharing everything with the natives by common consent." One metropolitan writer later called the Miçmacs "the legitimate possessors" of Acadia (Nova Scotia) and remarked that "these Savages defended with single-mindedness a territory which they hold from Nature. . . ."[38]

The case of the Abenakis makes even more clear the French dependence upon the so-called Allied Nations. It also clarifies the difference between French and British concepts of aboriginal title. The Abenakis learned the terms of the Treaty of Utrecht (1713) from the British, who said that the French "after having used them to wage war," made a separate peace without consulting them whereby they ceded their lands to the Queen. The Abenakis refused to believe this until some English showed them the precise treaty terms. What followed is recorded in a French memorandum of the period:

> Then the Abenakis became angry and demanded to know by what right the King of France disposed of their country. Their anger would have gone farther had they not been quietened by the Missionaries who told them they were being deceived by equivocal statements and that their lands were not included in what had been ceded to the English.[39]

Three years later, some English settlers attempted to assert their property rights to Abenakis lands along the Atlantic coast and the St. John River region on the pretext that the French had ceded Acadia. The Abenakis were quick to react:

> But the natives answered that this land had always belonged to them, that they were not subjects of the French but only their allies and their friends, that the French could not have ceded to the English lands that belonged to the savages, and that they would not quit them. They were right to say that the French are only their allies, the Marquis de Vaudreuil always having addressed them in that manner so as not to be held responsible for their deeds.[40]

In 1722, the missionary Rasle reported that two English traders had set up truck houses for the Abenakis, after having purchased the right to do so, but when settlers joined them the Abenakis asked by what right they settled on native lands:

> The answer which they received, that the King of France had ceded their country to the King of England, threw them into the greatest alarm; for there is no Indian nation but suffers most impatiently what they regard as subjection to any other power, whatever it may be; they term them indeed their allies, but nothing more.[41]

They made grants without any thought of alienation of lands, but with the idea simply of extending the rights and privileges to others which they themselves enjoyed on ancestral lands given them by the Great Spirit. The French understood this concept and did not offer payment for lands appropriated. Both parties seem to have taken for granted that the lands belonged to the Abenakis who acknowledged the French King and received his missionaries and so automatically came under French sovereignty. The English, on the other hand, appear to have maintained the paramount claim in the Crown and, while admitting the aboriginal rights of the Abenakis, to have sought to obtain releases through purchase or treaties.

The French position was based in good measure on their peculiar military relationship with the Amerindians. The Abenakis were essential to the defence of Canada, playing the role of a buffer between the two European areas of settlement. A memorandum to Versailles explained the situation in these terms:

> 1. that this nation is the sole bulwark of the colony against the English or the Iroquois.
>
> 2. that if we do not agree or do not pretend to agree to their rights over the country which they occupy, never will we be able to engage them in any war for the defence of this same country which is the first line of defence of Canada.[42]

The French claim to the Great Lakes region, and to the loyalty of its tribes, was founded on the same distinction between French sovereignty and Amerindian possession and independance. A memorandum of 1755 explained the situation as follows:

> In 1671, all the Peoples of the North, of the West and the South

> adopted the King of France as their Father and their Sovereign, and declared themselves to be his faithful subjects. M. de St. Lusson, sub-délégue general at Montreal, went to visit their coasts, received their homage and took once more solemn possession of their country.[43]

The French might interpret this as a quasi-feudal submission, but the Amerindians would see it as a formal declaration that they voluntarily became His Most Christian Majesty's children inasmuch as their traditional rights were being respected.

VI

The French system of reserves, as has already been suggested, was a special aspect of inter-racial relations. The reserves as originally perceived in 1637 were designed to assist in the integration of Amerindian and French populations. The objective was to attract nomadic hunting and food-gathering tribes to designated seigneuries administered by the missionaries in proximity of French colonists in order to introduce the Amerindians to a sedentary, disciplined, agricultural Catholic community life. At the outset the reserves were inter-tribal and included traditionalists as well as Catholic converts. The Jesuits operated the Sillery reserve near Quebec and Prairie de la Madeleine reserve near Montreal, while the Sulpician secular priests had a reserve near Ville-Marie called La Montagne. The lack of assimilation into proximity of French society, the slow pace of conversion, the evil influences of the proximity of French settlements, and especially the ravages of the brandy traffic imposed some fundamental changes on the reserve system. The reserves tended to move away from close contact with French settlers and the chief towns—thus Lorette replaced Sillery, Sault au Récollet and eventually Lac des Deux Montagnes replaced La Montagne, while Sault St. Louis or Caughnawaga replaced Prairie de la Madeleine. Later reserves, such as the Abenakis reserves at Bécancourt and Saint François and the Missisiquoi, la Présentation and St. Régis reserves were even farther removed from the centres of French population and acted as buffers along the frontier with the English colonies. The reserve became an institution of segregation, or at least of gradual acculturation in relative isolation from the towns and seigneuries of Canada.

The uniqueness of the French reserves is demonstrated in the motives various natives had for settling there, or remaining on them when return to ancestral homelands was a viable alternative. The Hurons at Lorette were remnants of the four Huron nations that had once lived in the region where the Récollets and Jesuits had started their Utopian interior mission. They were originally refugees from the Iroquois invasion of Huronia. Similarly, some of the Abenakis who settled on reserves south of Trois Rivières were refugees from New England expansion into their lands. Others, notably Iroquois converts, came to Sault St. Louis or Lac des Deux Montagnes as refugees from persecution and discrimination in their traditionalist village. The Iroquois council at Sault St. Louis told the Governor in 1722:

> The first and sole motive which made us quit our country and our families was Religion. We sought a place to make it secure among us and in imitation of our Missionaries we found no better place than near the French.[44]

There were some, on the other hand, who fled to the safety of the reserve because they had been accused of witchcraft in their village–the missionaries received them willingly saying that "the devil unwillingly becomes the occasion of the salvation of these wretched fugitives by making it less difficult for them to embrace Christianity."[45]

The reserves also augmented their members through adoption of prisoners. These might even include New Englanders, especially women and children, who not infrequently would not return to their relatives when the French arranged prisoner-of-war exchanges and offered to redeem them from adoptive families on the reserve. A missionary at Caughnawaga reported as follows in 1741:

> Our Indians are always at war with the Chicachas, and from time to time they bring in a good number of slaves; but instead of retaliating by burning them at the stake, they adopt them in the village, instruct them in the mysteries of religion, and by holy baptism place them in a way of reaching heaven.[46]

The reserves were not without economic attraction to some enterprising individuals and families. Gifts of food, clothing and arms were regularly distributed on the reserves and when canoemen, guides and interpreters were required the French turned first to the reserves for assistance which was well remunerated. At Sault St. Louis and Lac des Deux Montagnes the illicit fur trade which developed between Montreal and Albany merchants, and which may have siphoned off about one-third of the peltries of New France between 1710 and 1750s, was an important source of employment for the "domiciled savages".[47] The legal situation was that Amerindians could only be stopped from carrying furs to Albany and luxury and trade goods back from northern New York in the interest of Montreal merchants; the natives were free to trade in their own interest with anyone, and the French *habitants* since the foundation of the colony could trade freely in New France, the monopoly being on the export of furs through the Company stores. The mission Iroquois were the principal intermediaries in this substantial Albany trade and their missionaries were widely believed to support their initiative. The Montagnais and Hurons at Lorette turned to selling moccasins, snow-shoes, sashes, fur caps and mittens, collars of porcupine quills, bows and arrows and paddles at the Quebec market towards the end of the French régime.

Satisfactory economic rewards tended to make loyal military allies. The domiciled tribes, as they were called, made up an important contingent in all of the chief French military expeditions. They participated not only in frontier raiding on English settlements, but also in long range expeditions such as the war against the Chickasaws in the Carolinas. The reserves became veritable military bases, which served as a buffer to protect the French and their domiciled Amerindians from surprise attacks from the south and also as liaison posts to maintain the neutrality of the neighboring tribes under British rule. The French found themselves obliged to maintain the reserves, at considerable and increasing costs, even after it became apparent that the initial objective of assimilation into a French lifestyle was proceeding only very slowly.[48]

The reserves never made French-like peasants of the Amerindians. At Lac des Deux Montagnes, for example, the Nipissings and Algonkins, who were nomadic hunters, left their village to hunt each winter and they were soon joined by the Iroquois of the same reserve, who though originally semi-sedentary horticulturalists showed little more interest in farming. The proximity of the forest of the Laurentides was reassuring to the Lorette families who, although their acquisition of cows and the growing of wheat and rye in addition to their traditional maize, beans, pumpkins and sunflowers showed some progress in agricultural skills, were able to sell the produce of their hunting, trapping and fishing at Quebec. The reserves were successful in the measure that they permitted a continuation in some ways of the traditional occupations and skills.[49]

Eventually, the French Crown made it a cardinal principle in dealing with the tribes of the hinterland, where seigneurial concessions were prohibited, to discourage any relocation and concentration of the Amerindians in proximity of the forts. Royal instructions in 1755 were very specific on this matter:

> There is still another principle established quite a long time ago in Canada, and which His Majesty remarks is followed on all occasions. It is to withdraw the savage nations from the places they have chosen to inhabit and draw them near the French posts. The trade motive had contributed more than anything else to this way of thinking and acting. In general it is a very poor use of His Majesty's funds and the authority and credibility of the commandants to encourage these kinds of migrations. The allied savages must be deemed well everywhere . . . and Sieur de Vaudreuil must leave to certain nations the liberty to wander and go about the lands of the colony, provided that they do not receive foreigners; for that last point is the most essential.[50]

The fiasco of Cadillac's plan to establish a number of villages near Detroit, far from habitual hunting grounds, near to the French and to other tribes, and readily accessible to English traders had not been without its lessons. The reserves continued throughout the French régime to have a positive role in the relationship with the domiciled natives within the seigneurial tract and along the international frontier, but it was not an institution deemed to be universally applicable or advantageous in New France.

VII

The French contact was significant in the measure in which it promoted or accelerated an evaluation and criticism of metropolitan French society. This critique culminated, in a sense, in the French Revolution. The Baron de Lahontan, who gave a soldier's view of the New World, had a fictional chieftain named Adario satirize the illogicalities of Catholic beliefs and the vices of European society. Similarly, Claude Buffier concocted a dialogue in which the artificiality and boredom of civilized life were stressed, while at the same time native life was portrayed as being free and happy. Maubert de Gouvest also, in his *Lettres Iroquoises*, had his factitious Igli write from France to Alha in Iroquois country urging a critical reconsideration of the earlier favourable impression of the French. Alha was asked to consider whether "these men are worthy of the sublime idea which our illustrious Iroquois had formed of them" and was advised to assure the Iroquois that "they are themselves the Sages of the Earth."[51]

Jean-Jacques Rousseau has been associated widely, and somewhat erroneously, with the myth of the Noble Savage. Rousseau never suggested that Frenchmen should or could return to the Iroquois level of human organization. Nevertheless, he gave one of the clearest statements of the thesis that self-perfection in the individual led to all manner of evil in the human species. He concluded:

> The more one thinks about it, the more one finds that this state was the best for man. . . . The example of the savages, who have almost all been found at this point, seems to confirm that the human race was made to remain in it always; that this state is the veritable prime of the world; and that all subsequent progress has been in appearance so many steps toward the perfection of the individual and in fact toward the decrepitude of the species.[52]

Grasset de Saint-Sauveur, on the basis of similar assessment. doubted very much that Frenchmen should persist in attempting to civilize the native peoples:

> Such are the mores of a people too often calumniated by travellers; in the depths of his wilderness, he [Amerindian] is adroit, laborious, intelligent, virtuous, a faithful friend, good husband and good father. What would he be were philosophy to discipline his soul and manners? . . . Perhaps he might stand to lose: he would become disciplined (*policé*) but corrupted.[53]

Even the missionary-traveller, Father P.F.X. Charlevoix, conceded that the liberty which the Amerindians enjoyed compensated sufficiently for the deprivations and inconveniences which characterized their life-style. These were as much reflections on a Europe burdened with its own complexities, controls and class divisions, as statements that primitive peoples exhibited naturally many of the virtues civilized men sought to cultivate.

Pierre Poivre attempted in 1722, while refuting de Pauw's thesis of colonial degeneracy, to assess the predominant French impression of Amerindian societies. He wrote:

> It follows from all that I have said above, that the soil and terrain of America, far from being degenerated, are virgin and generally better than those of our hemisphere; that the natural and exotic products are good and abundant; that the prodigious quantity of animals and plants have kept men there for a longer period in a savage way of life, through the facility they have enjoyed in clothing and feeding themselves: that the savages are certainly inferior in intellect and in learning to Europeans; but that they possess no less good sense, or reason than they; and that they are generally as robust, as brave, and much happier.[54]

Such a statement is valuable to the historian in indicating both the understanding and the prejudice, the sympathy and the ignorance, of a well-informed man of the Age of the Enlightenment.

VIII

The purpose of this paper was to set out the unique features of the French contact with the Amerindian peoples in the period from first recorded contact through to the end of French rule in North America, with special emphasis being placed on the 18th century experiences. It does not come as a surprise that this experience played a role in the emergence of a theoretical framework for the social sciences concerned with native peoples, the concept of civilization, and the evolution of societies in a pattern sometimes called progress. It was in part out of the reported nature of North American native societies that Turgot conceived and formulated his Four Stages theory of progression from hunting and collecting economies through pastoralism to agricultural societies, and eventually to sophisticated commercial and industrial societies. His lectures in the late 1740s at the Sorbonne developed the thesis that human societies progressed through successive stages according to their mode of subsistence, not according to different modes of political organization or some other kind of "life cycle."[55] Algonkian society, accordingly, could be regarded as a living model of human society in the first stage of its development, while Iroquoian society was already more "progressive"–an assessment with which the missionary Joseph François Lafitau would agree. This hypothesis that all mankind progressed through the four successive stages of development, with the "savage" being the most primitive mode of life, was adopted eventually by Lewis H. Morgan in his *Ancient Society*. Both Friedrich Engels and Karl Marx relied heavily on Morgan's assumption that social evolution was universal, unilinear, automatic and progressive. This theory of social evolution according to which no country can skip any important phase in its industrial development was important in the formulation of the "mode of production" concept.

Our chief concern, however, was not to establish some direct linkage between contemporary social theory and the interpretations of early French contact with native peoples. One cannot help remark, nevertheless, the overwhelming Europocentric view of history and of the world which Frenchmen had. They placed themselves at the centre of the universal stage and judged other societies by the measure of their own. Be that as it may, in the French experience in America we catch sight of another spirit as well–one of cosmopolitanism and humanitarianism. This spirit manifested itself eventually in the Declaration of the Rights of Man and in such acts as the abolition of slavery. The French seem to have believed in their *génie colonial*, although it may have been more imagined than real, and in doing so they espoused a benevolent universalism.

What also emerges from this overview is the dynamism and vitality of Amerindian cultures at the time of contact. The Amerindians were free and independent peoples, willing to adjust to new circumstances, and sufficiently dynamic to deflect certain intruding elements of European civility to their own advantage. European and Amerindian societies were very different, each having some positive things to learn from the other. Neither saw the other as its ideal; yet neither saw the other as worthless.

The French contact experience is probably not a model of good race relations for contemporary Canada. On the other hand, the elements that have been singled out as unique contain some useful lessons for our times. There remains a need for clear and consistent policies. More attention needs to be given to peaceful coexistence and to historic rights. There is still need for greater self-criticism and the acknowledgement that we are not at the apex of human development, but that we are in the words of the 18th century writers only in the "infancy of the world."

NOTES

1. Michèle Duchet, *Anthropologie et histoire au siècle des lumières* (Paris, 1971), pp. 194-199, 279; Cornelius de Pauw, *Recherches Philosophiques sur les Américains* (Berlin, 1768), Vol. I, pp. 55-56, 61-63; Sieur Duret, *Voyage de Marseille à Lima et dans les autres lieux des Indes Occidentales* (Paris, 1720), pp. 261-262; Pierre Chaunu, "Laa légende noire antihispanique," *Revue de Psychologie des Peuples* (1969), pp. 188-223. The tradition had been established in France as early as 1667 by the Dominican missionary Jean-Bapliste du Tertre, author of *Histoire génerale des Antilles habitees par les Français*, 4 vols. (Paris, 1661-7).
2. Huntingdon Library, Vaudreuil Papers, Letterbook I, Vaudreuil to Maurepas, 1 June 1744, p. 260; P.F.X. de Charlevoix, *Histoire et description generale de la Nouvelle-France, avec le Journal historique d'un Voyage* (Paris, 1744), p. vii; Public Archives of Canada (hereafter P.A.C.), MG 18, H-27, Félix Martin Papers, Description of Hudson Bay and Strait by Jérémie, p. 196; J.F. Bernard, *Relation de la Louisiane, et du Flauve Mississippi* (Amsterdam, 1720), p. 10.
3. *Lettres de la Marquise de Pompadour, 1753-1762* (Londres, 1773), Vol. I, p. 149.
4. J.P. Brissot de Warville, *Nouveau Voyage dans les Etats-Unis de l'Amérique septentrionale fait en 1788* (Paris, 1791), Vol. II, pp. 429-430.
5. Citations from Francis Parkman, *The Conspiracy of Pontiac* (New York, 1962), p. 169; Sylvie Vincent and Bernard Arcand, *L'Image de L'Amérindien dans less manuels scolaries de Québec* (Ville La Salle, 1979), p. 188.
6. Anoymous, *The Expediency of Securing our American Colonies* (Edinburgh, 1763), p. 57; Thomas Mante, *The History of the Late War in North-America* (London, 1772), p. 479. Professor Herman Merivale's lectures at Oxford on colonisation in 1839-41, published in 1861, contained the following assessment of the French contact: "No other Europeans have ever displayed equal talents for conciliating savages, or, it must be added, for approximating to their usages and modes of life."
7. Georges Hardy, *Histoire de la colonisation française* (Paris, 1931), p. vii; André Julien, *Les Voyages de découverts et des premiers établissements* (Paris, 1948), p. 182; Hubert Deschamps, *Les méthodes et les doctrines coloniales de la France* (Paris, 1953), p. 16.
8. Francis Parkman, *The Jesuits in North America in the Seventeenth Century* (Toronto, 1899), Vol. I, p. 131; Philip Means, *The Spanish Main* (New York, 1965), p. 197; Mason Wade, "The French and the Indians", in H. Peckham & C. Gibson, eds., *Attitudes of Colonial Powers toward the American Indian* (Salt Lake City, 1969), pp. 61-79.
9. See our "Conceptual Frameworks for French Views of America and Amerindians," *French Colonial Studies*, No. 2 (1978), 1-22 and "L'Amérique vue par les Français aux XVIe et XVIIe siècles," *Rapports, XVe Congrès International des Sciences historiques* (Bucarest, 1980), II, 272-278. Also, Lewis

Hanke, *Aristotle and the American Indians* (Chicago, 1959). 44-73 and *The Spanish Struggle for Justice in the Conquest of America* (Boston. 1965). 111-131.
10. Donald M. Frame. ed., *Montaigne's Essays and Selected Writings* (N.Y., 1963). p. 89.
11. André Thévet, *Less Singularitez de la France antarctique, autrement nommée Amérique* (Paris, 1555), p. 51.
12. Olive P. Dickason, "The Concept of *l'home sauvage* and early French colonialism in the Americas," *Revue francsaise d'histoire d'outre-mer*, t. LXIII, No. 234 (1977), pp. 5-32; Archives Municipales de Saint-Malo, Série HH, Carton I, 1; Samuel de Champlain, *Voyages et Découvertes faites en la Nouvelle-France* (Paris, 1620), p. 1.
13. Cited in Michèle Duchet, *Anthropologie et Histoire au siècle des lumières* (Paris. 1971), p. 246. Our translation into English.
14. Georges-Louis Leclerc, Comte de Buffon, *Oeuvres complétes* (Paris, 1824-29). XV, 445-6.
15. Cornelius de Pauw, *Recherches philosophiques sur les Américains* (London, 1770). Vol. I. pp. 35, 221; Vol. II, pp. 102, 153-154.
16. Guillaume-Thomas-Francois Raynal, *Histoire philosophique et politique des établissement des Européens dans les deux Indes* (Paris, 1820-21), Vol. IX, p. 25. Cf. Arnold H. Rowbotham, "Jesuit Figurists and Eighteenth Century Religion," *Journal of the History of Ideas*, Vol. XVII, No. 4 (October 1956). pp. 482-3.
17. Raynal, *Histoire philosophique*, IX, p. 23.
18. Thomas Mante, *The History of the Late War in North-America and the Islands of the West-Indies* (London, 1772), p. 56. For a full treatment of the subject consult Harry M. Ward, *"Unite or Die": Intercolony Relations, 1690-1763* (Fort Washington, 1971).
19. Fernand Grenier, ed., *Papiers Contrecoeur et autres documents* (Québec, 1952). La Chauvignerie to Saint-Pierre, 10 Feb. 1754, pp. 100-101 gives a good account of such as occasion.
20. Stanley Pargellis, ed., *Military Affairs in North America, 1748-1765* (New York. 1969), Thomas Pownall's Consideration of 1755, p. 165.
21. *A.C.* (Paris), Série C11B, IV, *abbé* Gaulin to Seminary of Foreign Missions, 17 November 1719, fol. 251v.
22. *P.A.C.*, MG7, I, A-2, Fonds français, Ms. 12015, Mémoire de Le Maire, 1717, p. 83.
23. *P.A.C.*, MG1, Série C11G, Vol. 3, Raudot to Minister, 12 November 1707, p. 272; Thomas Mante, *The History of the Late War in North-America and the Islands of the West-Indies* (London, 1772), p. 97.
24. *P.A.C.*, MG4, C2, Vol. 3, Mémoire sur l' état présent du Canada, 1730, p. 12.
25. Harold A. Innis, *The Fur Trade in Canada: An Introduction to Canadian Economic History* (New Haven, 1930) should be considered in the light of W.J. Eccles, "A Belated Review of Harold Adam Innis, *The Fur Trade in Canada*." Canadian Historical Review (1979). *A.C.* (Paris), Séries C11D, VI, Subercase to Minister, 20 December 1708, fols. 166-166v; H.G. Davies, ed., *Letters from Hudson Bay, 1703-40* (London, 1965), p. 136.
26. Pierre Dolivier, *Essai sur la justice primitive* (Paris, 1792), p. 17; Morelly cited in Paul Hazard, *European Thought in the Eighteenth Century* (Cleveland, 1967), p. 177.
27. Lorenzo Angers, *Chicoutimi, Poste de Traite (1676-1856)* (Montreal, 1971). Coquart to General Murray, 12 March 1765, p. 60.
28. General Montcalm made this claim in 1762, writing about "an uninhabited land which may be considered to have been abandoned", applying it to all of

New France. *P.A.C.*, MG18, K7, Papiers Montcalm, Extraits de mémoires, 1762.

29. Emmerich de Vattel, *Le Droit des Gens; ou, Principes de la Loi Naturelle* (Washington, 1916), Vol. III, p. 38. On the right conferred by discovery see J.P. Kimney, *A Continent Lost — A Civilization Gained. Indian Land Tenure in America* (New York, 1975), p. 4. Cadillac thought prior discovery conferred no more title than would the discovery of a star: *P.A.C.*, MG5, B1, Vol. VII, Cadillac to Duke of Orleans, 1720, p. 152.
30. Cited in Peter A. Cumming and Neil H. Mickenburg, *Native Rights in Canada* (Toronto, 1972), p. 79. It should be noted that most of the ideas about native land tenure are based on comparatively recent ethnographic studies, not on the original historical sources of the XVI-XVIIIth centuries. Cf. Ralph Linton, "Land Tenure in Aboriginal America," in O. Lafarge, ed., *The Changing Indian* (Norman, 1943), pp. 53-54.
31. Pierre Margry, ed., *Découvertes et établissements des Français dans l'ouest et dans le sud de l'Amérique septentrionale* (Paris, 1888), Vol. VI, Journal de la Vérendrye, 1743, p. 609.
32. Moland, ed., *Voltaire: Oeuvres. Moeurs des Nations* (Paris, 1877), Introduction, p. 19.
33. F.X. de Charlevoix, *Journal of a Voyage to North-America* (Ann Arbor, 1966), Vol. I, p. 380.
34. *P.A.C.*, MG1, Série C11A, Vol. I, Extracts from diverse relations, 1646-1684, p. 427.
35. *P.A.C.*, MG1, Série C11E, Vol. II, Memorandum on establishment of Missions among the Iroquois, 12 November 1712, pp. 27-28.
36. *A.C.* (Paris), Série B, Vol. 89, Rouillé to La Jonquière, 4 May 1749, fol. 67; *P.A.C.*, MG5, B1, Vol. 24, Discussions on limits of Canada, 9 May 1755, p. 354.
37. *P.A.C.*, MG18, E-29, Discourse of St. Ovide, n.d., n.p.
38. De la Roche-Tilhac, *Almanach Amèricain, ou Etat physique, politique, ecclésiastique et militaire de l'Amèrique* (Paris, 1784), p. 420.
39. *P.A.C.*, MG18, H-27, Papiers Félix Martin, Memorandum on Acadia and the Abenakis, p. 236.
40. *P.A.C.*, MG1, Série C11A, Vol. 36, Vaudreuil to Duke of Orleans, February 1716, p. 125.
41. W.I. Kip, ed., *The Early Jesuit Missions in North America* (New York, 1846), Sebastien Rasle to nephew, 15 October 1722, p. 10.
42. *P.A.C.*, MG18, H-27, Papiers Félix Martin, Memorandum on Acadia and the Abenakis, p. 235.
43. *P.A.C.*, MG4, C.1, Article 14, Vol. 1, No. 5, Rights of French Crown in Canada, 1755, p. 33.
44. *P.A.C.*, MG1, Série C11A, Vol. 106, Memorandum of the Missionaries of Sault St. Louis, 12 May 1722, p. 113.
45. Arthur E. Jones, ed., *The Aulneau Collection, 1734-1745* (Montreal, 1893), Nau to Bonin, 2 October 1735, p. 64.
46. *Ibid.*, Nau to Mme. Aulneau, 3 October 1741, p. 140.
47. *P.A.C.*, MG1, Série C11A, Vol. 33, Vaudreuil & Bégon to Minister, 12 November 1712, p. 56; MG1, Série F3, Vol. pt. 1, King to Vaudreuil & Bégon, 8 June 1721, pp. 168-69.
48. *P.A.C.*, MG1, Serie C11A, Vol. 35, Begon to Minister, 25 September 1715, pp. 273-75.
49. *P.A.C.*, MG18, K-5, Papiers Franquet, Vol. II, Voyage from Quebec. 1752, pp. 61-64.
50. H.R. Casgrain, ed., *Extraits des Archives* (Quebec, 1890) Royal instructions to

Vaudreuil, 1755, p. 33.

51. Baron de Lahontan, *Conversations de l'Auteur de ces Voyages avec Adario sauvage distinque* (Montreal. 1974); Claude Buffier, *Cours des Sciences sur des principles nouveaux pour former le language et le coeur dans lùsage ordinaire de la vie* (Paris, 1732), pp. 954-57: J.H. Maubert de Gouvest, *Les Lettres Iroquoises* (Paris, 1962),
52. Jean-Jacques Rousseau, *Second Discourse* (New York, 1964), Pt. 2, p. 151.
53. Jacques Grasset de Saint-Sauveur, *Moeurs, Loix et Coutumes des Sauvages du Canada* (Paris, 1788), p. 8.
54. Pierre Poivre, *De l'Amerique et des Americains, observations curieuses du philosophe La Douceur* (Berlin, 1722), p. 114.
55. G. Schelle, ed., *Oeuvres de Turgot* (Paris, 1913). Vol. I, pp. 255-274.

2

THE EVOLUTION OF NATIONALISM IN FRENCH CANADA

Ramsay Cook

I

To the outsider and even to its own citizens contemporary Canada presents a striking paradox. Its two dominant political figures are both French-speaking Quebecers. One, Pierre-Elliot Trudeau, the prime minister of Canada, is uncompromising in his conviction that Canadian federalism provides the surest guarantee for the future of French Canadian culture. The other, René Levesaué, premier of Quebec, holds with equal fervor the conclusion that only in a politically sovereign Quebec will French-Canadian – or as he would prefer, *Québecois* – culture be assured of healthy growth.

To add to that apparent paradox, most observers of Canadian affairs over the past twenty years would agree that Quebec has been the prime instigator in the recent efforts to revise the Canadian constitution. While most English-speaking Canadians, during these past two decades, regarded the constitutional issue as more of a nuisance than a priority, French-speaking Canadian leaders have insisted that constitutional revision was the country's most pressing need. Yet, when the new Canadian constitution was finally proclaimed in 1982, the representatives of the Quebec government were vociferously absent. English Canadians mainly heaved a sigh of relief – the constitution was finally made completely Canadian with an amending process that made further requests for amendments by the British parliament unnecessary. Moreover, a Charter of Rights and Freedoms, including entrenched guarantees for the French language and minority educational rights, had been included in the new fundamental law of Canada. Wasn't that what Quebecers had wanted? The answer of many French Canadians, especially but not only those who supported René Lévesque *Parti Québecois* government, was negative. Indeed, the Quebec premier charged that he had been betrayed, not only by his old enemy Pierre Trudeau, but also by the other provinces who, together with Quebec, had for months, even years, prevented a resolution of the constitutional deadlock by refusing to agree with Ottawa's proposals. Moreover, Lévesque argued, the new constitution rather than meeting Quebec's constitutional demands actually weakened that province's position within the Canadian federal system. His conclusion was that, more than ever the need for complete political independence was obvious.

Who spoke for Quebec? The question, as always, was impossible to answer categorically. Prime Minister Trudeau, the principal architect of the new constitution, could claim that since his party held virtually every federal seat in Quebec, his new constitution had the support of Quebecers, René Lévesque, whose party held an overwhelming majority of the seats in the Quebec legislature, could, and did, make the same claim. These counter claims were hardly new, for they reflected accurately the curiously contradictory performance of the Quebec voters over the previous decades. Let me review some of the most obvious elements in this picture.

Since 1968 Canada's federal government at Ottawa has been presided over by Pierre-Elliot Trudeau and a cabinet in which the dominant voices have often been French Canadians. During these years Prime Minister Trudeau's party, the Liberal party, has grown stronger and stronger in Quebec, currently holding all but one seat in that Province. Many of the Trudeau government's major policies – the enactment of the Official Languages Act and the promotion of the use of French in the public service, the establishment of closer relations with the French-speaking world, regional economic development and even energy policy – could be interpreted as being in significant part designed to meet the need of Quebec. "French power", as French-speaking members of parliament enjoyed reminding their voters, had become a reality. Nevertheless, eight years after Trudeau first won office and set out implementing politics designed to eradicate the growing independence movement in Quebec, René Lévesque's *Parti Québecois* won an overwhelming election victory on 15 November 1976. Levesque's platform called for the establishment of a politically sovereign Quebec which would negotiate a somewhat undefined economic association with English-Canada – with the Atlantic provinces as East Pakistan or Bangladesh, Ontario and the west as West Pakistan, Quebec would become the new India, lying between the two.

Lévesque's nationalist movement is an exceedingly cautious one, bearing almost no real similarity to the nationalist movements of the Third World with which it occasionally liked to associate itself. Knowing that only a minority of Quebecers – perhaps no more than 15 or 20% – favored complete independence, the *Parti Québecois* advocated not only economic unity with the rest of Canada, but it also promised that before it took any steps towards independence it would consult the electorate in a referendum. That cautious policy was known as *etapisme* or independence step-by-step, so gradual that whatever pain or cost it might entail would be little more than a minor irritant.

A referendum was held in May 1980. The people of Quebec, in a skilfully devised question, were asked if they would give their government a mandate to enter into negotiations with Ottawa with the object of gaining for Quebec political sovereignty combined with economic association somewhat along the lines of the European Common Market.

Prime Minister Trudeau and the federal Liberals (back in office after a brief nine months leave-of-absence during which the Conservatives, with virtually no support from Quebec, held power), joined in the battle advocating a defeat of the referendum question. Sixty per cent of Quebecers voted "non", forty per cent responded "oui". The *Parti Québecois* had absorbed a major setback, even though something close to fifty per cent of the French-speaking voters supported the affirmative. (About eighty per cent of the Quebec population is French-speaking, the remaining twenty per cent of "Allophones" have English as their predominant language, though they come from many ethnic backgrounds.) Despite the rejection of the *Parti Québecois's* primary objective, the Quebec voters one year later, in April 1981, returned Premier Lévesque to office for another term, once again with a large majority of seats in the National Assembly. In that election Lévesque promised not to hold another referendum during a new period of office, though the party remained committed to eventual independence, perhaps without economic association if necessary.

In the period between the referendum and the Quebec provincial election. Prime Minister Trudeau, in keeping with the promise he made during the referendum that if Quebecers voted "no" to the Lévesque question he would press for a renewed federalism, reopened negotiations with the provinces. Those negotiations which were complex and often bitter and involved a major decision by the Supreme Court of Canada, ended finally in agreement late in 1981 – agreement that is of Ottawa, and all of the provinces except the Province of Quebec. That constitution was proclaimed with much fanfare in Ottawa in April 1982. In Quebec City the legislature adjourned in a day of mourning, and the Premier led a public demonstration against the new constitution. Canada, as usual, was without unanimous agreement.

At the end of twenty years of public debate and negotiation, the answer to the question of Quebec – and Canada's – future remained a long way from resolution. In Ottawa, Pierre-Elliot Trudeau's Liberals, strongly supported in Quebec remained in power, committed to a constitution that makes French and English equal languages in public business and, within certain limits, in education within a federal system that accepts Quebec as one of ten equal provinces. In Quebec City René Lévesque's *Parti Québecois*, equally firmly supported by the Quebec voters, continues to promote a unilingually French-speaking society which, the Parti Québecoisr hopes, will ultimately achieve full sovereignty, not as one province among ten, in a Canadian federal system, but rather as one nation among hundreds in a world of equal nations. The apparent *impasse* continues, and will do so until Quebecers are able to do what they have never done in their past – conclusively make up their collective mind.

My purpose is not to comment further on these contemporary matters, but rather to look, as an historian should, at the background to those events in an effort to explain the apparent paradox of Quebec posed as it seems in a fine balancing act unwilling or unable to chose its future definitely. When the complexity of Quebec's history and position in North America is examined, its ambiguity appears much more understandable.

Let me turn at once then to the past in an effort, once more, to decipher the riddle of the sphinx *qui parle francais*.

II

1840 was a grim year for French Canadians. Papineau abortive rebellion and its aftermath left the *canadiens* profoundly pessimistic, Durham's *Report*, recommending assimilation, had an air of finality about it. Union with Upper Canada, as the essential first step, was about to be forced on Lower Canada. So bleak was the future that Etienne Parent, the most brilliant political writer of his generation and editor of the nationalist *Le Canadien*, declared his acceptance of assimilation if that was the price necessary to gain responsible government.[1]

In that depressed atmosphere of 1840, two *Canadien* artists set down, one in poetry the other in paint, their convictions and feelings about the future. In doing so they provided two enduring clues to the well-springs of nationalism among French Canadians. The poet was Francois-Xavier Garneau, later to become famous as an historian. In 1840 he published "Le Dernier Huron", a poem about a people who had been defeated, dispersed and assimilated.

> Their names, their eyes, their celebrations, their history, Are with them scattered forever.
> And I remain alone to speak of their memory
> To people to-day![2]

The Hurons, of course, stood as symbols for *Canadiens* wno, Garneau feared, would share the fate of that once proud and powerful Indian nation.

An Indian also served as a symbol of French Canada in Joseph Legare's 1840 painting entitled *Paysaqe au Monument a Wolfe*. Here we see the Indian apparently offering to surrender his bow to the statue of the conqueror, General James Wolfe. Yet nearby, hidden behind a tree trunk, is a canoe waiting to carry the Indian away to his freedom. The critics seem agreed that the Indian (a Mercury figure) is more cunning than submissive, and that he is really preparing to escape to the freedom and independence of the forest.[3]

Taken together these two works of art symbolize the psychological dimension of nationalism among French Canadians. The last Huron is the nightmare of ultimate extinction. Legare's deceptively submissive Indian represents the dream of complete freedom. After nearly a century and a half, neither the nightmare nor the dream has come true. But they remain part of the French Canadian nationalist psyche, as the psychiatrist-turned-politician, Dr. Camille Laurin, has often noted.[4]

Fear of the future, fear of extinction can be traced to at least two sources. The first is historical. Defeat, something shared by Amerindians and *Canadiens*, is a central part of the French Canadian historical experience. In the beginning was the Conquest. Each generation of French Canadians study, reinterpret and try to come to terms with this central fact of their history, and of all Canadian history. Yet it never goes away. Here is a passage from the Lévesque government's recent statement of policy on Quebec cultural development. It is a lengthy passage but it is a perfect summary of the currently dominant view of the Conquest among Quebec nationalists.

> Then the Conquest came. A small population having had at its disposal a relatively brief time to implant itself firmly on its territory, the original Canadians had to turn in on themselves and assure themselves of the foundations of their survival and of their development in a country firmly taken in hand by another people whose language, religion, laws, political institutions and genius were foreign to them. A conquered group, politically and economically dominated, the Canadians little by little developed the sentiments of a minority and became progressively marginalised in a country which was formerly theirs, but whose commanding heights had quickly escaped them. Regrouping themselves, chiefly in the rural areas, they clung to the soil, to their language, to their religion, to their way of life. As a result of the conquest, they became isolated as businessmen from the great North American trade and have thus been rendered rather impermeable to the great revolutions of the Western World; they have been satisfied to endure, anchored in the solid realities which form the basis of peasant life.[5]

Mach of the *Parti Québecois's* major public documents takes that sense of defeat symbolized by 1759 as its point of departure, once again demonstrating the centrality of the conquest to nationalist thought.[6]

Consciousness of a second defeat has assumed an increasingly prominent place in the ideology of contemporary Quebec nationalism: the failure of Papineau's rebellion in 1837-38. In the past Papineau's anti-clerical side lessened his attraction to clerical nationalist writers. But today, in a secular Quebec, he has been rehabilitated and the *patriotes*, even though they failed, have gained a new responsibility. "One hundred and thirty years ago," Robert Lionel Seguin has written, "the patriotes of Saint Denis showed us the road of dignity and liberty. Fertile seed from which we gather the fruit today."[7]

To the conquest and the abortive rebellion of 1837 other familiar defeats are often added: Piel's hanging, Manitoba Schools, Regulation 17 in Ontario, Conscription in two world wars, even the Air Traffic Controller's crisis of 1976 when the use of French in the air space over Quebec was temporarily prohibited. Victories, when they come, are always too late: the Supreme Court of Canada rejected some restrictions on English in Quebec less than three years after enactment; a Manitoba law abolishing French waited ninety years for the same result. A history filled with defeats and humiliations must surely stimulate pessimism. "The only issue – a more or less long term issue," a Montreal historian wrote in the 1950s "is the assimilation of the weaker culture by the stronger." And yet that pessimistic nationalism was closely linked with the rise of separatism in the 1960s, and its historical interpretation is part of the official ideology of the *Parti Québecois*.[8]

Fear of the future has a second underlying cause: numbers. Throughout their history French Canadians have been preoccupied with their minority position. That is hardly surprising. New France was a tiny colony, outnumbered even by its Huron allies in the 17th century and constantly overshadowed by the more heavily populated English Colonies to the South. While the French outnumbered the English in the Canadas until the 1850s, the pressure of English-speaking immigration was a major influence in the growth of the *parti patriote* in the 1830s.[9] One of the themes that runs constantly through Garneau's *Histoire* is his fear of a future in which the *Canadiens* will be a minority. Again and again he refers to "un peuple peu nombreux", "un peuple si faible en nombre" and so on. "But a people that is not numerous," he observed in explaining the French Canadians' attitude during the American Revolution, "cannot control its own destiny, is obliged to observe many precautions and much prudence."[10]

Throughout the latter half of the 19th century French Canadian leaders were extremely conscious of two demographic facts. The first was "the revenge of the cradle." An extraordinarily high birth rate meant that French Canadians fulfilled the Malthusian law: population doubled every twenty-five years. "During the last two centuries," a Quebec demographer wrote in 1957, "world population has been multiplied by three, European population by four, and French

Canadian population by eighty, in spite of net emigration which can be estimated at roughly 800,000.[11] Given those figures even Sir John A. Macdonald's view that the solution to the French Canadian problem lay in immigration and copulation sounds futile.

But the other half of the demographic picture for French Canadians was emigration, chiefly to the United States. That "national haemorrhage" quite understandably obsessed French Canadian leaders form the 1840s to the early 20th century.[12] While some optimists thought that these southbound waves of Roman Catholics would one day restore puritan New England to the true faith,[13] the more frequent reaction was fear – fear that Quebec's population losses would be English Canada's political gain. *Abbé* J.B. Chartier put the issue very bluntly when he declared that only "traitors" rejoiced at the sight of Quebecers moving to the United States; keeping them at home was "a question of life and death for the French Canadian race."[14] The 19th century campaigns of Cure Labelle, Arthur Buies and others to colonize northern Quebec, and Canada, were conducted in the fulsome rhetoric of providential mission, but the goal was a very worldly one: to keep French Canadians at home where their heads could be counted by census takers and vote gatherers.

That preoccupation with numbers has not declined in the slightest. Nowhere in Canada is the decennial census scrutinized more thoroughly than in Quebec. In the last twenty-five years Quebec Francophones have fully absorbed the values and aspirations of urban-industrial people everywhere. That has been accompanied by a dramatic decline in the birth rate. In 1961 Quebec's leading demographer, Jacques Henripin, speculated about population trends in Canada. If existing immigration rates remained constant and French Canadians continued to adopt English at the 1961 rate, he predicted that by 1981 only 23.5 per cent of the Canadian population would be French-speaking, and that percentage would fall to 17 per cent by the year 2011. In 1951 the percentage was 29 per cent.[15] That statement, cautious and careful as it was, set off a chain reaction that led directly to Bill 101, the Charter of the French Language, in 1977. But before that stopping place had been reached the language issue had proven its potency: in St. Leonard something near communal strife erupted between Francophones and immigrants anxious that their children learn English. Both the *Union nationals* of Jean-Jacques Bertrand and the Liberal administration of Robert Bourassa fumbled the issue. And that played a significant part in the election victory of the *Parti Québecois* in 1976. In the midst of these events the Gendron Commission produced a massive report in which a convincing case was made for making French the working language of the province. The Commission's conclusion was: "This policy does not represent a false concern with the problem of numbers. It is clear that the falling birth rate of French speakers, together with the slight attraction that the French language exercises on the non-French speaking constitutes a subject of legitimate concern for French-speaking Quebecers. The fear that French-speaking people will become a minority, if it is unfounded inside Quebec, is much more valid on the Canadian level."[16]

"The fear of becoming a minority": there is the heart of the matter. It is in fact the leitmotif of much Quebec nationalist writing from Garneau through to successive policy statements of the Lévesque Government. It was central to the White Paper on Language policy where one bold-faced sub-heading summed up the issue: "If the demographic evolution of Quebec remains constant, Quebecers will be less and less numerous". The same point is underlined in the opening pages of the cultural development policy statement and, inevitably, forms a central part of the argument for sovereignty-association. In the *Parti Québecois* Government's White Paper *La Nouvelle Entente Quebec-Canada* two large graphic illustrations dramatize the following information: in 1851, 36% of Canadians were Francophone; in 1971 that figure was 28% and by 2001 it will drop to 23%. That in turn means that Quebec, which in 1867 held more than one-third of the seats in the Canadian House of Commons, will by 2000 hold less than one-quarter. "Under these circumstances", the authors of the White Paper argue, "it would be an illusion to believe that, in future, Francophones can play a determining role in the Government of Canada. On the contrary, they will be more and more a minority and English Canada will find it increasingly easy to govern without them. In that respect, far from being an anomaly, the Clark government is a sign of things to come."[17]

By encouraging "the fear of becoming a minority," the Last Huron syndrome, the Lévesque government hopes to convince Quebecers that the time has come to choose independence, to fulfil Joseph Legare's vision of freedom. That theme, too, runs deeply in Quebec history. From the resort to arms in 1837 to Lévesque's proposed New Deal in 1979, the hope for independence has always remained alive among small groups of Quebecers. For the most part it has never been much more than a dream to be achieved someday. After Papineau's defeat the dream of separate nationhood lived on in a segment of *le parti rouge* which opposed Confederation in 1865, (as did a few *bleus*, including the young Honore Mercier). What the *rouge* favored in 1865 was not complete independence but a loose form of federalism in which the member states would remain sovereign. When the Quebec Resolutions passed the Canadian Assembly (27 French Canadians in favour, 22 opposed), a newspaper of *rouge* persuasion fulminated: "On this memorable night has been committed the most iniquitous and degrading act which the parliamentary system has witnessed since the Irish deputies sold their country to England for positions, honours and gold."[18]

Like much else in Quebec in the latter part of the 19th century, the idea of independence gradually acquired a clerical and conservative tone though its origins with the *rouges* had been secular and liberal. Its chief exponent, Jules-Paul Tardivel, (his enemies called him Jules-Paul Torquemada after the head of the Spanish Inquisition), edited a newspaper characteristically called *La Verite*. In the 1880s, Riel's execution and Macdonald's centralizing policies convinced him that only independence would save Quebec from Anglo-Saxon Protestant domination. In his utopian novel, *Pour la Patrie* published in 1895, he described the events which, with God's help, led to independence in 1945. One passage, explaining the nationalist goal, is especially interesting:

> Our geographical position, our national resources and the homogeneity of our population enable us to aspire to be ranked among the nations of the earth. It is possible that Confederation offers certain material advantages, but from the religious and national point of view it is filled with dangers for us, for our enemies will certainly manage to wear it away until it is a legislative union in everything but name. Moreover the chief material advantages that are derived from Confederation could be obtained equally well through a simple postal and customs union.[20]

In addition to the obvious similarities to sovereignty-association as devised by the *Parti Québecois*, Tardivel's projected *Republique de la Nouvelle-France* contains some other revealing details. Most notable was the assumed peaceful manner of its achievement – no revolution, no civil war, just a rather heated parliamentary debate, in which a sympathetic English Canadian Catholic played a crucial role. René Lévesque's plans are postulated on a similar assumption. Canadians, he believes, are sufficiently civilized to be able to work out a division of their country in a federal-provincial conference, presumably carried on prime time television with suitable commentary.

Those who kept the light of Quebec independence alive during the generations that followed Tardivel were equally reasonable in their expectations. In 1922 Canon Lionel Groulx and his friends in *l'Action francaise* published an enquiry into *Notre Avenir Politique* which concluded that the future was unfolding, as expected, towards independence. But it would come as a natural evolution "as soon as Providence wishes it."[21] French Canadians were called upon to prepare themselves, but the timetable was unspecified. So, too, the young separatists who joined with Andre Laurendeau in *Jeune Canada* in the late thirties spoke only in terms of an undefined future when, by undefined means, "one day a country will be born."

Until the 1960s, then, when *Le Rassemblement pour l'Independence nationale* and later the *Parti Québecois* were born, the ideal of independence was simply that, an ideal, more perhaps a state-of-mind than a concrete political project. Yet it is impossible not to be struck by the degree to which the *Parti Québecois* fits into this tradition of ambiguity and caution. Independence by steps: *etapisme*. Not even Mackenzie King, that Canadian master of ambiguity, of never doing things by halves that could be done by quarters, could have improved on the Lévesque-Morin strategy. First the removal of the independence issue from the 1976 election by the promise of a referendum. Then a definition of independence that is not independence but sovereignty-association. Next a referendum asking not for approval of sovereignty-association, but merely a mandate to negotiate. Finally a promise of yet another referendum on the outcome of the negotiations. Everything is hedged. Is it any wonder that a radical separatist like Pierre Vallicres, in frustration, has pronounced the *P.Q.* strategy "as ineffective in liberating Quebec as the improvised revolt of the Patriotes of 1837-38."[23]

Why is nationalism in Quebec so cautious in tactics, so modest in its demands? Legare's Indian may be preparing to escape into freedom, for the canoe lies ready. Yet he is also in the act of surrendering his bow to the statue of Wolfe. Perhaps it is not Mercury after all but rather, as the playwright Robert Gurik once contended, Hamlet who is *Prince de Quebec*.[24] If as I have been arguing, French Canadian nationalism is driven by a fear of extinction, on the one hand, and the dream of absolute freedom, on the other, then it is driven in contradictory directions. Fear of the future and hope for the future combine to create indecision, ambiguity, paradox. Is that not Papineau, brilliantly characterized by Fernand Quellet as *A Divided Person*, and by Garneau as "the image of our nation?" Caught between the desire to preserve and the desire to liberate, between nationalism and liberalism, he was paralysed, a Franklin without being a Washington.[25] Is that not also René Lévesque?

Garneau himself expressed that same tension which is at the heart of French Canadian nationalism. At the conclusion of his great *Histoire*, having surveyed the struggles of his people from the first arrival of the explorers to the union of 1840, he drew one last lesson. It is often quoted, and rightly so, for it catches as nothing else does, the essential character of nationalism in Quebec:

> Let the Canadians be faithful to themselves:
> Let them be wise and persevering, let them not be seduced by the brilliance of social and political novelty. They are not strong enough to follow a career of that sort. It is for great nations to test new theories: they can move freely in their spacious orbits. For us, part of our strength comes from our traditions; we must not stray far from them and alter them only gradually.[26]

That sense of prudence, that belief in the need to tread carefully and to be guided by past traditions, has continued to characterize French Canadians throughout their history. And it is against the background of modest, but persistent, nationalism, that the goals of Quebecers can best be understood, whether expressed in the demand for equality of linguistic rights, special powers for the province of Quebec, or sovereignty-association.

But simply the goal of French Canadians has always been security, the strategy for its achievement is the recognition of equality. For a self-conscious minority, both the goal and the means of achieving it, are perfectly understandable. By definition a minority is potentially at the mercy of the majority. It lacks security. It must discover a way to maximize its position, to find a mechanism that will allow it to act as an equal or near equal. Consciously, or otherwise, this has always been the strategy of French Canadians anxious to preserve their national distinctiveness. And that includes virtually all French Canadians for, though they have often been divided on means, they have never been divided on ends.

What strategies are possible and available? Papineau tried one route: equality established through independence. That is the tradition of *d'eqal a'eqal*, the *Parti Québecois* call to arms. But the lesson that many of Papineau's followers drew from the rebellion's failure was that equality would have to be achieved within a political system that they shared with other Canadians. Such equality might never be perfect, but it would be attainable. That was the central message of L.H. LaFontaine's address to the Electors of Terrebonne in 1840. He demanded, and received, an equal share of power within the Union: that was what the Rebellion Losses Bill demonstrated. But the primary symbol of his success was the repeal of the prohibition against the use of French that had been part of the original union constitution. He practised what Canon Groulx admiringly called "a national policy"[27] by convincing French Canadians to stand united behind him and thus to maximize their strength. This is the strategy of "French Power" practised by every successful French Canadian federal politician since Cartier: by the concentration of the minority's votes in one party it becomes a near equal.

It is not a perfect strategy and, since it has resulted in defeats as well as victories, critics have devised alternatives. The primary one, historically, might be called "fortress Quebec". It stands between "French Power" and separation, taking something from each. It argues that since French Canadians will always be a minority in the federal system, they should concentrate their talents at the provincial level where they are a majority. Quebec, as the homeland of French Canadians, should thus be recognized as a province *pas comme les autres* with powers, at least in some areas, equal to those of the federal government or of all the other provinces combined. This strategy was practised in a limited manner by Mercier in the 1880s, and by Duplessis and Lesage in more recent times. The report of the Tremblay Commission on Constitutional Problems in the late 1950s worked out this theory most completely. And variations on the theme of "fotress Quebec" – though offering fortress status to other provinces, to – can be found in M. Claude Byan's recent proposal for *A New Canadian Federation.*[28]

Underlying each of these strategies is a conception of French

Canada and/or Quebec as a distinctive society, a nation in one of several senses, deserving equality with other nations and particularly with its partner, English Canada. That equality is seen as a necessary condition for the security that alone will banish the Last Huron nightmare, and fulfil, at least in part, Legare's dream.

III

Discovering the formula that will guarantee Francophones security through equality has been the persistent quest of Quebecers for nearly two centuries. The very vitality of Francophone culture today is testimony, surely, to the degree of success that French Canadians have achieved. Neither Garneau's fears nor Legare's hopes have been fulfilled. Both possibilities remain, and so does the riddle on the face of the French-speaking sphinx.

The ambiguity remains because it is an accurate reflection of the reality of Quebec society, its hopes and its fears. But it is more than that. It also reflects the shrewdness of a small, determined people who have discovered over the centuries that in the end survival depends on themselves, and that no single strategy is perfect. Where some see ambiguity as a sign of weakness – "cultural fatigue"[29] the brilliant novelist, Hubert Aquin called it, – others, and I think correctly, judge it more sympathetically. "The French Canadians frequent duality of allegiance," Michel Morin and Guy Bertrand conclude their dissection of the public philosophy of Quebec, "wheroby they elect a federal or a provincial government, testifies sufficiently to the natural intelligence of the people, to individuals anxious to guarantee their liberty and their rights, by opposing one to the other the princes who govern them."[30]

NOTES

1. Jacques Monet, *The Last Cannon Shot*, (Toronto, 1969), 25.
2. J. Huston, ed., *Le Renertoire national*, (Montreal, 1893), 1, 172-5.
3. Francois-Marc Gagnon, "The Hidden Image of Early French Canadian Nationalism: A Parable", *Arts Canada*, December 1979-January 1980, 11-14.
4. Camille Laurin, *Ma Traverse du Quebec*, (Montreal, 1970), 85.
5. *La politique quebecoise du developpement cultural* (Quebec, 1978), I, 50-51.
6. *Quebec-Canada: A New Deal*, (Quebec, 1979), 3-4.
7. Robert-Lionel Sequin, *La Victoire de Saint-Denis*, (Montreal, 1964), 45; Marcel Rioux, *La Question du Quebec*, (Paris, 1969), 70-71.
8. Michel Brunet, *Canadians et Canadiens*, (Montreal, 1954), 30. Maurice Seguin, *l'idec de l'independence au Quebec*, (Montreal, 1968).

9. Fernand Quellet, *Le Bas Canada 1791-1840*, (Ottawa, 1976), 214ff.
10. F.X. Garneau, *Histoire du Canada*, (5th edition, Paris, 1920), II, 392; Philippe Reid, "Francois-Xavier Garneau et l'inferiorite numerique des Canadens Francais, "*Recherches Sociographiques*, XV, 1, 31-39.
11. Jacques Henripin, "From Acceptance of Nature to Control: The Demography of the French Canadians Since the Seventeenth Century", *Canadian Journal of Economics and Political Science*, XXIII, 1, February 1957, 10-19.
12. Yolande Lavoie, *L'emigration des Canadiens aux Etats-Unis avant 1930*, (Montreal, 1972).
13. E. Hamon, *Les Canadiens-Francais de la Nouvelle Angleterre*, (Quebec, 1891), 155-56.
14. Christian Morissonneau, *La Terre Promise: Le Mythe du Nord Quebecois*, (Montreal, 1978), cited 78.
15. Jacques Henripin, "Evolution de la composition ethnique et linguistique de la population canadinne", *Relations*, XXIe annee, 248, aout 1961, 207-09.
16. *La Situation de la Langue francaise au Quebec*, I, *La Langue de Travail*, (Quebec, 1972), 301.
17. "La Politique quebecoise de la Langue francaise", *Le Devoir*, 2 avril, 1977. 7; *A New Deal*, 29-30.
18. J.P. Bernard, *Les Rouges*, (Montreal, 1971), cited 265.
19. Fernand Quellet, "Nationalisme canadien-francais et Laicisme au XIXe Siecle", *Recherches Sociographiques*, IV, 1, janvier avril, 1963, 44-70.
20. Jules-Paul Tardivel, *For My Country, Pour la Patrie*, (1895), (Toronto, 1975), 39. Translation by Sheila Fishman.
21. *Notre Avenir Politique*, (Montreal, 1923), 29.
22. Andre Laurendeau, *Notre Nationalisme*, (Montreal, 1935), 50.
23. Pierre Vallieres, *Un Quebec Impossible*, (Montreal, 1977), 71.
24. Robert Gurik, Hamlet, *Prince de Quebec*, (Montreal, 1968).
25. Fernand Quellet, *Louis-Joseph Papineau, Un Etre Divise*, (CHA Booklet, Ottawa, 1961), cited 22.
26. Garneau, *Histoire*, 33.
27. Lionel Groulx, "Un Chef de trente-trois ans," in *Notre Maitre, le Passe, le Passe,*, (2Ieme Serie, Montreal, 1936), 150.
28. *A New Canadian Federation*. The Constitutional Committee of the Quebec Liberal Party, 1980, 12.
29. Hubert Aquin, "The Cultural Fatigue of French Canada", in Larry Shouldice, *Contemporary Quebec Criticism*, (Toronto, 1979), 55-82.
30. Morin et Bertrand, *Le Territorie imaginaire de la culture*, (Montreal, 1949), 154-55.

3

FEDERALISM AND PROVINCIAL AUTONOMY AS DEVICES OF IMPERIAL CONTROL

Partha Sarathi Gupta

By the time Britain had effectively established its paramount power in India, ruling about one-third of the subcontinent directly, and, influencing, in imperial interests, the policy of the remaining two-thirds (the princely states), imperial necessity had established certain minimum levels of administrative and economic unification of India. In British India, to give but a few examples, the civil and criminal codes, railway policy, and the free movement of trade within British India were testimonies to that. The great vested British interests which together comprised the authority that felt vulnerable to opposition from Indians were the British expatriate businessmen in India, the British exporters to India, the City of London which was concerned about the servicing of the Indian debt, the British bureaucracy in India, and the British army in India.[1] Opposition to British domination could come from social groups with a limited local perspective or from groups which, for reasons of ideology and or self-interest, developed an all-India nationalist perspective. For the British Raj, political success lay in defeating the latter. Whether at the local or at the all-India level such opposition sometimes reflected social forces which could be accommodated within the framework of colonialism by modification of priorities within the British interests mentioned above, or social forces which were far too hostile to be so accommodated. These latter were either direct challenges to a whole group of British interests or subversive of the social order which permitted the operation of colonialism.

It is by now a truism that in the period after 1917 the imperial power was more vulnerable than before and to maintain authority constitutional adjustments had to be made along with a reshuffling of priorities. Among these we notice administrative devolution, provincial autonomy, and the federation of component units. These are themselves politically neutral. They can often help to strengthen the sense of national feeling in a geographically large or culturally pluralist state, as in Canada, Switzerland, or Belgium. In the context of colonial rule, however, they were conceived of as an attempt to deflect all-india challenges to British authority. Many conservative British officials who heartily disliked even the small concessions to the principle of responsible government and elected assemblies conceded in 1919, were pursuaded to accept the reforms because it made them relatively free to develop their own techniques of encouraging loyalist elements in their own localities: "provincial autonomy", liberal as it was, smacked of divide and rule.[2] Yet imperial dominance had derived its maximum economic and political advantage from the unification of the subcontinent. As these new techniques were used there were frequent queries from British interests about their relative fortunes in the new dispensation. Would the constitution be able to keep out of the corridors of power any all-India party which did not recognise the legitimacy of British rule or the imperial claim to decide when, how and if at all power should be totally transferred?

This paper will examine the approach to provincial autonomy in the period after 1927, till the outbreak of war brought in a new situation. It will analyse two of the contradictions within colonial interests that were revealed in some detail, the problem of transferring the law and order portfolio and the distribution of the income tax between the centre and the provinces. After a brief account of the period till 1931, we shall concentrate on the four years when the Government of India Act (1935) was in the making, and conclude with some observations on how far the calculations of the conservative imperial power had been successful. The eight years that intervened between the appointment of the Simon Commission and the passage of the Act of 1935 were characterised by the world economic crisis, political and agrarian agitation in India, three changes of government in Britain (1929, 1931, and the defections of the free-trade Liberals in 1932), and the end of free-trade and international gold standard in Britain. The constitution was put into effect in British India against the background of threats of war in both Europe and Asia. So, in the last resort, protecting the constitution could only be done by political goodwill. Military force was limited. As Lord Reading, former Viceroy and Liberal politician, put it to J.R. MacDonald, urging him to make a success of the second Round Table Conference,

> If we fail, then it will be a case of troops and money from here, when we can spare neither and when we shall be preoccupied with our own financial and economic troubles.[3]

I

The Government of India Act (1919) had transferred only three departments–education, local self-government, and health–to elected ministers, and had left other crucial portfolios like Finance and Home to the imperial bureaucracy. At the centre there was a legislative assembly entitled to vote on the budget but the viceroy could restore any cuts imposed by it. In both the centre and the provinces a group of officials sat in the assemblies with the right to vote and support the government's side. Many officials did not like this role, this being not part of their training, but in terms of imperial requirements there was no alternative.

When the Indian Statutory Commission was appointed in anticipation of the decennium of the Act of 1919, a cross section of Indian political opinion, ranging from the Indian Liberals, to some groups of Muslims and the Congress, boycotted it, and set about drafting an alternative constitution. This constitution, known as the Nehru report (after Motilal Nehru, its Chairman) preferred a unitary constitution for the whole of British India. On the other hand Muslim politicians preferred to have a federal constitution with residual power to the provinces. The pros and cons of federal and unitary systems in India in the colonial period had as a result been focused as if it was essentially a difference between politicians with different religious affiliations. How much of federalism and how much of central control suited the imperial authorities has not been subjected to critical scrutiny.

The extensive boycott of the Simon Commission ensured that it heard evidence only from regional and minority groups. Its report also took no notice of all-India political nationalism. By recommending no change at the centre it followed the tradition of 1919, but it conceded provincial autonomy subject to special powers for the governors. By the time the report was published in June 1930, the advent of the Labour government in Britain and the heightened tempo of the civil disobedience movement led by Gandhi had made Viceroy Lord Irwin realise that sharing some powers at the centre with business groups and moderate politicians (involving some concessions at the expense of specific British interests) was the only guarantee for controlling the Civil Disobedience Movement.[4]

The first Round Table conference accepted the principle of a federation of autonomous British provinces and princely India, leaving details of the federal structure to be worked out by subcommittees. On some major issues all-India unity was possible, like the rapid Indianization of the Indian army and the freedom of the federal assembly to decide the customs revenue. Before the second session, the Labour governmental had fallen, to be succeeded by the National Government. It was to this second session that Gandhi came, but was unable to make any headway against the combined opposition of the European expatriates and Muslim leaders like the Aga Khan.

In the National government the conservatives were in a majority. The coalition character of the government was carefully maintained by both MacDonald and Baldwin, and cabinet discussions were often very prolonged as a result, but the general election of the autumn of 1931 gave the Conservatives such a massive majority that henceforth their point of view on India and the empire held sway over the more liberal approaches of the previous government. The Tory Secretary of State for India, Sir Samuel Hoare, argued the case for provincial autonomy and the postponement of constitutional advance at the centre with the following points:

> . . . it has the strong support of the Minorities. The most significant feature of this antumns's discussions has been the consolidation of a single front by the Moslems, the depressed classes, the Christians, and the Anglo-Indians. There is a grave risk of our having no friends in India at all if we disregard the representatives of the 120 million Indians who have hitherto refused to take part in civil disobedience.[5]

This remained a dominant theme in conservative thinking. It was also supported by the European expatriate interests. Their representative Sir Edward Benthall, who had teamed up with the

Muslim communalist delegates at both Round Table Conferences felt reassured by Lothian's view that the relations between the provinces and the centre will be limited.[6] Pressure on MacDonald from the Indian Liberals, Lord Reading, and others ensured that the notion of a simultaneous advance at the centre was not abandoned officially, but as late as May 1932 Hoare was keen on going ahead with a bill in favour of provincial autonomy only, until finally dissuaded by Viceroy Willingdon.[7]

The concern for some advance at the centre as sketched out at the first round table conference was expressed by Willingdon and British liberals because, while putting down Gandhi's movement with a firm hand, they valued the support of the Indian liberals. If the Conservatives were happily contemplating the support of the minority groups, the Liberals were aware that without some advance at the centre, no cooperation would be forthcoming from business groups and from Indian liberals associated with them. The Liberal Lord Lothian, under-secretary of state for India, visiting India as Chairman of the francise committee, concluded that while civil disobedience had suffered a severe drubbing the 1919 constitution had "been under sentence of death for two or three years" and could not be revived. It was "really weakening everywhere." Only a firm promise of a new constitutional settlement which did not go back on the promise of a federal centre might really ensure support from the moderates.[8] Sykes, the Governor of Bombay, argued, "Ordinance basis of our rule in India cannot be continued indefinitely," and added a plea for federal centre where Britain would exercise strong financial control.[9]

On the other hand there was little sympathy with the idea of central control by the federal government in Hoare and Simon. In August 1932 MacDonald had been pursuaded to give the "Communal Award on the Franchise" question to satisfy the demands of influential Muslim groups in Punjab and Bengal, and whose case had been pleaded by Viceroy Willingdon.[10] To clinch the political advantage from this Hoare and Simon, on the eve of the second Round Table Conference took a strong line in favour of minimal central control on provinces. While discussing the draft constitution prepared for the cabinet committee in September 1932,[11] Hoare argued that "the general conception of the constitution ought to be that the centre of gravity should henceforth shift from the centre to the Provinces." Apart from administrative reasons, "there were more serious reasons in favour of the change. Considerations of imperial safety demanded a greater variety in the Indian picture than it now presented. When a solid mass of Indian interests was too often to be found in opposition to a solid mass of British interests; and it had become clear that the Moslem population of India would never accept the Reforms scheme if steps were not taken to ensure the reality of Provincial Autonomy. The unitary idea must be regarded as dead, although it was not always recognised by Indian opinion . . . ." Simon added that he hoped to see the extent of Provincial Autonomy so complete that the Federal Government would be denied all power of interference in Provincial subjects."[12] When the Reforms Commissioner J. Dunnett mildly suggested that there should be some proviso to secure uniformity of the great Indian legal codes like the penal code, Hoare, while not objecting to such technical details, reiterated that he "strongly opposed . . . any arrangement which perpetuated the present all-pervading influence of the Centre–that was a conception from which it was essential that the new Constitution should get completely away.[13] The official mind visualized that the special powers given to the Governor within the framework of responsible government and provincial autonomy, would enable imperial interests to be safeguarded: "The absence of organised parties, of vitality in the electorate, of homogeneity in the legislature and in the Cabinet, and of experience in the political executive accordingly suggest conditions favourable to the effective association of the Governor as an imperial partner in the work of government."[14]

During the preparation of the despatch setting forth the views of the Government of India during Lord Irwin's viceroyalty (the drafting committee sat from 25 June to 20 September 1930) the Punjabi Muslim leader Sir Fazl-i-Husain repeatedly clashed with some British officials (like Dunnett) who had pleaded, on administrative grounds, for some central control over provinces. Fazl-i-Husain also had been supporting leaving residuary powers to the units.[15] The government of India now began to reveal an inner contradiction, how to placate regional or communal anti-Congress groups while safeguarding imperial interests. This is revealed in the next two sections, where the question of the devolution of law and order and centre-province financial relations are discussed. As we shall see, the decisive factor in the centralist thrust was the cluster of imperial interests mentioned earlier and the opposition of Indians was brushed aside. There was no question of abandoning the reforms altogether though that would have pleased Winston Churchill and the Conservative die-hards. On answering a query of Stanley Baldwin about the draft constitutional proposals published in March 1933, Lord Brabourne, Governor of Bombay, wrote:

> I have taken great pains to find out what the ICS and Police officers in the Presidency really think of the White Paper proposals and in nearly every case their attitude can be summed up as a dislike of the whole thing but a firm conviction that it is much too late to go back now. Some of the younger Policemen are strongly against the whole policy but their line is that 'given enough police we can control any trouble in india'–which may or may not be the case but is hardly what we want.[16]

II

Law and Order

During the discussion in the summer of 1930, in course of arguing against extreme provincialism, James Dunnett had pleaded for some superintendence, direction, and control by the central government over the provinces. In some federal states, as in the U.S.A and Switzerland, there were federal agencies to execute federal laws, whereas in British India the practice so far had been to supplement the all-India services by using the provincial police force and similar bodies as agents of the central government. Expense alone ruled out the creation of mutually exclusive and completely self-sufficient federal and provincial bureaucracies. Against this Sir Fazl-i-Husain, apprehensive that a party might be in power at the centre which had a different outlook from that in a province, argued that such supervisory powers over the provinces should be at the personal discretion of the Governor-General, without any reference to the central legislature or the central government.

Since all parties present at the first Round Table Conference were agreed on making 'law and order' a provincial subject under a responsible minister, the imperial authorities were concerned about how to control classes of offences like terrorism and communism which could not be done without some control from the centre. Under the existing constitution, controlled by the bureaucracy, police administration in the provinces was divided between a political branch (which dealt with these issues) and a criminal branch which dealt with ordinary crime. The deputy Inspector-General of Police in charge of these usually dealt directly with the chief secretary of the provincial government. The entire funds were voted by the legislature. The existing Police Acts, passed long before there was any question of Indian participation in the legislative process, put the inspector-general of the police under the control of the provincial government. "A local government without any alteration of law, could, by unwise interference, reduce the discipline of the police." In attempting to prevent this and develop some concurrent jurisdiction over the police between the centre and the provinces the British Home Member Sir Harry Haig and Sir Fazl-i-Husain were once again on opposite sides. Haig did not like the supervisory powers over law and order in the person of the Governor-General and not the central government because then the latter might adopt "a merely critical attitude towards a policy for which they were relieved of all responsibility." (What worried Sir Harry was a recurrence of a situation like 1930 when, with only dominion status defined as a far-off goal, people could be mobilised for complete independence and the moderate nationalists would tend to sit on the fence.) Sir Fazl-i-Husain put in a strongly worded caveat at the end of this despatch:

> It appears to me that there is greater need for laying down in the constitution that the centre shall not interfere with the provinces than of inserting a provision that the province shall obey the order of the centre. . . . We cannot have provincial autonomy, and at the same time a centralised administration of law and order.

In October 1931, at the second Round Table Conference where, as we have seen, Hoare had started his tilt in favour of minority groups against the Congress, he asked Haig if it was not possible to eliminate the federal government altogether from the picture in the administration of law and order, giving the Governor-General personal powers like the U.S. President. Haig did not consider it practicable, and stuck to his original position. Loose supervisory powers "might have very far-reaching effects and would lead to centrifugal tendencies."[17]

In Bengal, the European expatriate businessmen were in a quandary over their general support to specific Muslim elite groups and their demand for the maximum measure of provincial autonomy, and their concern for their own safety from revolutionary violent groups. To the suggestion that complete provincial autonomy combined with no change at the centre would suit Britain best, Benthall countered that the "great majority of the security services in Bengal would forthwith resign and in six months the province would be lost. For twenty years Bengal had been run only with the aid of the C.I.D. which could not be maintained under the conditions visualised. . . ."[18] Both Lothian and Benthall about this time advised the Reforms Office to emulate the U.S.A. in developing self-sufficient federal bureaucracies for federal functions, especially taxation and police.[19]

It took nearly two years before the Conservative government in Britain, anxious to consolidate its support among the anti-Congress groups, took note of these fears of European expatriates and bureaucrats. Following the tradition of Fazl-i-Husain his successor in the conference Zafrullah Khan had added a note of dissent to a Reforms Office despatch of 16 July 1932 which suggested that the Federal government and the provincial governments should have some concurrent administrative jurisdiction over the maintenance of peace and tranquillity and over criminal legislation, control of arms and the press. Hoare supported Zafrullah Khan's alternative view that Governors-General and Governors, under their personal direction shoud do such task of coordination.[20] The conservative politician remained far apart from the Conservative bureaucrat. Haig sourly noted,

> I feel the Secretary of State has formed a picture of the Governor-General of the future as a Great Mogul, maintaining order throughout the country by his personal authority. . . . Unless we are going to allow the disintegration of India, there must be certain points with which both centralised and provincial legislature will be concerned.[21]

Hoare ignored this.

The initial balance struck between imperial interests and the conciliation of the autonomists was weighted on the side of the latter. The White Paper on Indian constitutional reform published in

March 1933 made police and law and order a provincial subject (no. 50 i list II), but not the point of Dunnett and Hague in putting criminal law and the code of criminal procedure in the concurrent list (no. 9 and 10). It was silent on the issue of the central co-ordination of intelligence on subversive activities and the follow-up action on that. As Hoare put it, to avoid appearing "provocative to provincial governments" the White Paper had avoided specific constitutional provisions requiring the provincial government to supply information to the federal government.[22]

London was aware that European expatriates, especially in Bengal, were worried about revolutionary violence, but how to provide a constitutional basis for controlling criminal intelligence behind the back of responsible ministers required a lot of ingenuity.

A cabinet paper put it lucidly,

> It is no exaggeration to say that most of the extreme politicians in Bengal are themselves connected with terrorist associations, and their news figure in the dossiers of the Intelligence Branch of the Presidency. (If ministers were) *constitutionally* . . . able to demand access to all their secret reports and to their dossiers . . . the advent of a Congress ministry in Bengal would necessarily entail the immediate destruction of existing dossiers; for otherwise the sources of information would be disclosed. . . . The very lives of the Agents depend on the safeguarding of their reports and of their identity. . . .[23]

The government of India and the provincial governments were prepared to let the provincial intelligence agencies come under the control of responsible ministers. The existing Central Intelligence Bureau was to be detached from the Home Department, attached to Defence or External Affairs (where funds were not votable by the Assembly) and have a few liaison officials in each province. From the imperial point of view its weakness was that a nationalist ministry could legitimately be able to so starve the provincial C.I.D. of funds that it was unable to follow up the centre's suggestions or could deem it just prudent not to cooperate with the central I.B. officials. The London officials' alternative scheme which they had not succeeded in getting into the White Paper, was embodied in the Government of India Act, thanks to the persistent lobbying of European interests in Britain. and Conservative constituency party organs.[24] Under this scheme, in each province the regular police and the criminal branch of the C.I.D. were transferred to the ministers but that part of the staff which did intelligence work on "All-India subversive movements" was to function as a direct agent of the Governor-General and have special liaison with the Governor.[25] The ideas were embodied in paragraphs 94-97 of the Joint Select Committee of the British parliament and enacted in sections 57 and 58 of the Government of India Act.[26] Imperial misgivings about the Inspector-General of Police falling under ministerial control which had been expressed earlier,[27] were allayed by requiring the Governor's prior consent before rules governing the Police Acts were amended.[28] The Central Intelligence Bureau was specifically mentioned in the Federal legislative list under "defence".[29]

The period between the publication of the White Paper and the Government of India Act, when a centralising thrust took place in European and imperial interests did not produce any noticeable backlash from politicians like Sir Fazl-i-Husain and Sir Zafrullah Khan, who had earlier been quick with their notes of dissent. The India Office also does appear to have taken their continued support for even the modified constitutional proposals for granted (in contrast to the Congress). This office had always felt that these politicians were exaggerating when they said that their safety depended on the lowest form of federal control because the Indian army had and was likely to have a majority of Muslims in it. An Indian Office note for the third Round Table Conference on centre-province relations had concluded by saying

> Moreover, it seems likely that by the time the Governor-General falls completely under the domination of his ministers, the Indian Army, as distinct from British troops, is likely to have passed under Indian control. So far as one can foresee, the Army will be predominantly Muslim, and is likely to be quite as powerful a factor in the Federation as any Hindu Executive and Legislature.[30]

III

Sharing of the Income-Tax

Provincial autonomy could be either a device for deflecting all-India nationalism in imperial interests or alternatively a training ground for self-government. In either case it involved different financial priorities. Between 1927 and 1935 the British government at first went a long way to provide elastic sources of revenue for its provincially oriented allies but then found that imperial interests (defence budget, home charges) required that these sources of revenue should be outside the control of self-governing provinces.

The settlement of the Government of India Act (1919) left the income-tax, an important elastic source of revenue, to the central government. There were repeated criticisms of this in the decade even from political groups who were not close to the Congress. Since these groups had given evidence before the Simon Commission, the latter felt obliged to state their point of view. Sir Walter Layton, the economist who advised the Commission recommended that fifty per cent of the income-tax should be available for distribution.

From the first Round Table Conference in November 1930 till almost two years after, the distribution of the income-tax was hotly debated, revealing a significant cleavage between imperial and local perspectives. The first draft of the constitution prepared by Lord Sankey towards the end of the Labour government had only done an outline financial chapter. At the second R.T.C. in September-December 1931, the financial subcommittee of the Federal Structures Committee, whose chairman was the Conservative Lord Peel, decided, under pressure from the Indians, in favour of provincializing the income-tax and making the central government dependent on provincial contributions. As Peel described the work of the committee at a Cabinet meeting which met to discuss the protests of the Government of India, "speaking privately, there had been a tendency throughout its deliberations to remove any and every source of revenue from the centre, for the benefit of the provinces. It had needed all his own efforts to retain for the centre what few sources of revenue he had in fact been able to save."[32]

Another committee under the Conservative statesman Lord Eustace Percy went into the details of the scheme, and recommended a modified form of provincialization of the income-tax. Both these proposals were political proposals designed to isolate radical nationalists and so they left some parts of imperial finances uncovered. The only way to convince London that the centre should have bulk of the finances (or at least a decisive say in its allocation) was to point to the danger to imperial interests: As the new Reforms

Commissioner W.H. Lewis wrote, "When financial safeguards are discussed, the point is fully emphasised that 80 per cent of the federal revenues are required for the military budget, debt, and pension charges, etc., for which parliament must take responsibility. The same emphasis is required when federal finance is under consideration."[33]

This argument was embodied in a long (36 pages, 96 paras) despatch in which the key sentence ran, "*The Federal Budget is therefore essentially a defence and credit budget, and thus must not be tampered with*" (italics in the original).[34] Probably because Sir Fazl-i-Husain had given a note of dissent to the government despatch, Hoare's initial reaction was to say that there might be more to be said for Peel's scheme.[35] However, by the middle of November 1932 Hoare had been won over by the financial interests in Britain. Peel pleaded for avoiding the mistakes of the 1919 reforms and giving the provinces elastic sources of revenue. Lord Percy added that "he was more inclined to trust Indians on finance than on any other subjects." Hoare replied that "this was far from being the view held in the House of Commons and the City of London, and the serious apprehension felt in these quarters would have to be taken into account."[36] Many British Indian delegates at the federal finance committee of this R.T.C. argued that the reduction of military expenditure will enable the federal government to be solvent without the income tax, and they reiterated that their claim for the right of provinces to levy a surcharge was not palatable to the Government of India, Hoare was unwilling to lose the political support of Indians who would cooperate. He kept the provincial surcharge.

The Act of 1935 left it all to an arbitral award by someone appointed by the British government to decide how much initial grant the provinces should receive on the eve of autonomy and how much would be the share of provinces in the income-tax.

Sir Otto Niemeyer's award arranged for a deferred payment of 50 per cent to the provinces, apart from providing minimum and fixed resources to each province to bear the expenses of the new constitution.[37] (The Government of India had wanted a permanent share of 60 per cent for the centre). Its effect was to limit the scope for expansion in army expenditure. It was a contradiction between the needs of imperial defence and the needs of imperial credit. Within an imperial framework no constitutional change could solve it.

The possibility of cuts in army expenditure had been noted earlier by the civilian wing of the British administration–Parsons in June 1932,[38] and J.B. Taylor (the future Governor of the Reserve Bank of India) in April 1933.[39] The Commander-in-Chief had warned against a cut of Rs. 15 crores because then the frontiers would be left defenseless, the princely states could not be helped, and the defense of the 3400 miles of railway security would be weakened. The "only sanction of law and order would be the goodwill of the people,"[40] and an imperial power could not afford to depend entirely on that. By Niemeyer's award the existing level of army expenditure was saved but the military authorities were ill-equipped to face imperial problems.

IV

Provincial Autonomy and Imperial Dilemma

During the debate on the report of the Simon Commission in July 1930 the Reforms Commissioner James Dunnett had noted, while making some calculations about the relative advantages of direct or indirect elections to the central legislative assembly, "There is something disquieting in the thought of a single all-India Party controlling the centre as well as the majority of the provincial governments in India."[41] Unfortunately for the future of the Raj the first general elections under the new constitution returned the Congress to power in five of the eleven provinces, and in Bombay also the Congress formed a stable ministry.* In the North-West Frontier province its allies the "Red Shirts" were in power. The bureaucracy now had limited options. If they succeeded in getting the princely states federate and send their nominees to the federal assembly, a much hoped for counterweight to the nationalists might emerge. If the provincial Congress ministers became preoccupied with local problems and acquired a mind of their own it was even better. Lothian hoped for this.[42] If on the other hand, before these had materialized fresh burdens were imposed in imperial interests then a breach between the government and the nationalists appeared very likely.

Assumption of office by the Congress had not resulted in any significant relaxation either by its rank-and-file or by its local leaders in their opposition to that part of the federal constitution whereby princes were to nominate the representatives. As the agitation against the princely states mounted in 1938 the Commander-in-Chief noted that the question of internal security was "likely to be just as serious if not more so than in the past."[43] The Home Member added that there was always the risk of simultaneous resignation of Congress governments and the inevitable use of emergency powers of direct administration laid down in the constitution. If such a thing happened it "would almost certainly be followed by some kind of civil disobedience on a much larger scale than has been experienced before" and would this time cover not only towns, but rural India. For this the British army was necessary.[44]

Faced with the difficulties of recruiting British soldiers the British War Minister proposed the reduction of four British battalions from those stationed in India. He also suggested that India maintained and paid for an imperial reserve division for operation east of Suez. The Government of India was concerned that the, "British element will be reduced by 30 per cent at a time when the political situation in India is far more threatening than it has ever been since 1857."[45]

Privately and in official despatches all authorities, including the die-hard finance member Sir James Grigg, gave reasons explaining why they could neither dispense with British troops nor afford to increase the army budget. In any case even without the costs of the Imperial Reserve Division, Hore-Belisha's pay-hike for British soldiers was going to add to Indian defense expenditure for that part of the British Army that was borne on the Indian list. The imperial authorities in India could just about manage that, out of the existing budget but no more. If the government wished its constitution to find fruition not only at the provinces but also at the centre, then, in the transitional period, with a Congress-dominated central legislative assembly, the safest thing was to transfer the burden of the imperial reserve defence to Britain.

The result of this deadlock was the appointment of the Chatfield Committee to consider if the British Government would contribute towards the cost of Indian manpower in imperial defense. The very fact that such a situation could arise was symptomatic of the failure to carry through the principle of federation and devolution before the nationalist party got bogged down with the details of provincial administration and lost its nationalist urge. Desperate efforts of

Linlithgow to get the princes to accede (which S.R. Ashton has recorded) did not succeed on the eve of World War II. The timing of the end of the British Raj in India, the nature of the elite groups who would be ruling the centre, the whole question of partition were now to depend on the worldwide social and economic upheavals caused by the World War II.

NOTES

(Unpublished Crown copyright records are quoted by permission of the Controllers of H.M. Stationery Office. Thanks are due to the Scottish Record Office for permission to use the Lothian papers, the Cambridge South Asia Centre for the Benthall papers, Churchill College archives for the papers of Sir James Grigg, the Cambridge university Library for the Baldwin papers, the Liverpool City Library for the papers of Lord Derby, and the Bodlean Library for the papers of the Conservative Party)

1. B.R. Tomlinson in *Political Economy of the Raj*. p. 27 mentions only three of these—the British exporter, the 'Home changes' and the use of Indian troops at Indian expense overseas.
2. R. Danzig, 'The many layered cake', *Modern Asian Studies*, VIII (1974). p. 64.
3. Reading to MacDonald, 28 Nov 1931 f. 6 (Macd. papers 30/69/698).
4. Irwin's remarks at the proceedings of the informal meeting of the Executive Council, 26 June 1930. (NAI—Reforms—Reforms—1939—file 67/V).
5. Note by Secretary, State for India for the Cabinet, 9 November 1931 (Cab 27/41 R.T.C. (31) 11.
6. Benthall to P.H. Browne, 23 October 1931 (Benthall papers, Box II, File 1931-32.
7. Cab 27/521 C.I. (32) nos. 5. 7. 8 and 11 for all the correspondence on this.
8. Lothian to Reading 25 February 1932 (GD 40/17/159 ff 21-22). In another letter of the same date of his cabinet colleague Sir John Simon Lothian said that the report of the Simon Commission itself had passed the death sentence on the Montford scheme (Ibid., ff23-25).
9. Sykes to Willingdon 11 April 1932 (Cab 27/521 C.I. (32) 9).
10. On this see David Page, *Prelude to Partition* (Delhi: 1982) and Robin Moore, *Crisis of Indian Unity* (Oxford: 1974).
11. The provincial part of the draft constitution had been prepared by Lord Sankey (who had been Lord Chancellor both in the Labour government and the National government) as early as 13 May 1932. (Cab 27/521 C.I. (32) 6. It was a slightly modified version of the one prepared during the tenure of the Labour government on 27 July 1931 (Cab 27.470 B.D.G. (31) 8).
12. Cab 27/520, C.I. (32) 12th Meeting of Cabinet Committee on India, 18 October 1932.
13. *Ibid*., 13th Meeting, 20 October 1932.
14. Cab 27/521 C.I. (32) 21 "Scheme of safeguards proposed and method of its operation", para 21.
15. NAI—Reforms—Reforms—1930. File 67/V/30. Proc. of 12th Meeting. 19 July 1930; Sir Fazl-i-Husain's note. 3 September 1930 (*Ibid*., file 67/x/30).
16. Brabourne to Baldwin. (Baldwin papers, vol 106 f. 348).
17. NAI—Reforms—Reforms—1930—file 67/VI.

18. Memo. of discussion at 37 Ballygunge Park, 18 February 1932. (Benthall papers, Box II, File 1931-32, item 26). Those present were Lord Lothian, Sir John Kerr, Edward Benthall, H. Carey Morgan, W.W.K. Page, E. Villiers & 'T.C.M.'.
19. Lothian to Dunnett, 9 February 1932; Benthall to Dunnett, 2 May 1932 (kept in NAI—Reforms—Reforms—1932. File 85/32).
20. Cab 27/521 C.I. (32) 29. Appendix, Secretary of State to Viceroy, 30 September 1932
21. Haig's Minute, 3 October 1932 (NAI—Reforms—Reforms—1932, F 014/32 keep with p. 15.
22. *Proposals for Indian Constitutional Reforms* (Delhi:1953), Para 114.
23. Cab 27/521 CI (32) 59 'Defence Security Intelligence', Paras 2 and 4.
24. The papers of Lord Derby, a member of the Joint Select Committee, and the resolutions of British Conservative Party branches testify to this.
25. As in note 23.
26. Government of India Act 1935, clauses 57 and 58.
27. See notes 19 and 20 above.
28. See relevant clause of the Act.
29. NAI—Reforms—General—1935—F 6/I/35, GIA, Secy of State to GOI P & J (c) 4774, 25 January 1955, para 28.
30. Cab 27/469 RTC (31) 4, India Ofice departmental not on communal and minority problems, 25 September 1931, para 8.
31. P.J. Thomas, *The Growth of Federal Finance in India* (Madras, 1939) ch xxx, passim.
32. Cab 27/520 CI (32) 27th meeting, 16 November 1932.
33. Lewis to Schuster, 12 May 1932, kept in NAI—Reforms—Reforms—1932 File 125/32 k.w., p. 4.
34. Despatch to Secy of State, 13 June 1932, para 6 (NAI—Reforms—Reforms—1932 File 123-32).
35. Cab 27/520, 27th meeting, 16 November 1932.
36. Indian Round Table Conference (2nd session), *Proceedings* of Federal Structures Committee and Minorities Committee, Vol. I (Calcutta, 1932) paragraphs 4, 5 and 6.
37. Niemeyer to Grigg, 23 October 1935 (PJGG 3/1/13 (d) (29).
38. Note by Parsons, 2 June 1932 in Reforms—Reforms—1932. File 123 kw, p. 4f.
39. Note by J.B. Taylor, 7 April 1933 in Finance—Finance 1933—File 17 (23)-F.
40. GCI to Secy of State 15 May 1933, Appx VII in *ibid.*
41. NAI—Reforms—Reforms—Secret Notes 1930, no. 31.
42. Lothian to Halifax, 3 May 1937 (GD 40/17/37, f 439-40).
43. I.O.R. L/WS/1/153, file W.S. 1931. f. 23-4,
44. *Ibid.*, f. 26.
45. Cab. 6/6 198-D para 10.

4

REGIONALISM AND FEDERALISM : THE CASE OF WESTERN CANADA

Carl Bercer

It is a commonplace that Canada consists of five distinct regions–the Maritimes, Quebec, Ontario, the Prairie West, and British Columbia. It is also a convention that the Prairie West has not only been one of the most clearly demarcated regional entities but that it has been the most restless and impatient with its subordinate position in the federal system. The main feature of the region is its geographical isolation from the rest of Canada–separated from the more populous central Canada by some two thousand miles of thinly settled rock and forests, and from the Pacific coast by a belt of mountain ranges five hundred miles wide. Physical isolation nourished a feeling of psychological separateness: the sense of enstrangement from the central government, however, was due more to policy and historical experience than to distance.

Unlike any other settled part of Canada, the Prairie West was the creation of the federal government. The acquisition of the north-west territories was one of the primary objectives of the movement to unite the British North American colonies and at Confederation the central government was given pre-eminent powers over economic development. From the formal purchase of the territory from the Hudsons' Bay Company in 1870 until 1930 the federal government administered and developed the area as a "colony" of the new Dominion. The main objective of a series of policies was to promote immigration and dense agricultural settlement; the protective tariff of 1879 was designed to promote industrial development in central Canada and give that industry a captive market on the plains. One of the purposes of the transcontinental railway was to integrate the economies of east and west–carrying immigrants, settler's effects, and manufactured commodities westward, and the wheat staple to the ports of eastern Canada for export. The development of western agriculture was not an end in itself; it was the instrument by which the entire national economy was to be activated and integrated in a commonalty of interests.

These national policies provided only the framework for western development: the actual stimulus to agricultural settlement depended upon favorable changes in the international economy which occurred in the mid-1890s. Though some settlement had taken place in the parklands earlier, the occupation of the treeless prairies in depth occurred in a remarkably short time between 1896 and the Great War and this took place in a spirit of incautious, heady optimism. When the surveyors of the federal government divided the land uniformly into townships and quarter-sections they impressed upon the new society one of its chief characteristics. The chief inducement/s to immigration--and the basic unit of prairie society--was the 160 acre free homestead given to any male settler who was a British subject to the fulfilment of minimal obligations. This settlement pattern dispersed the population on isolated farms and proved very costly in terms of providing basic social services. The whole enterprise was, in fact, a gamble. Little was known with any certainty about the weather patterns and variation in soils across the prairies, and the attitude of the federal authorities seemed to be that settlers would sort themselves out and learn by their mistakes. The failure rate in this process was high: over the whole settlement period over 40 per cent of those who entered upon a homestead failed to secure title for it. Those who succeeded and upon whose initiative depended the creation of schools, churches and other institutions were in no mind to fatalistically accept things as they were.

The economy that had come into being by 1914 was based on highly specialized wheat production for the international market. It was not only vulnerable to shifts in price in that market but also at the mercy of unpredictable weather. This monolithic economy supported a society that possessed a high degree of class homogeneity: some 60 per cent of the population was directly involved in farming and the remainder in one major and several minor cities and in the hundreds of villages and hamlets that were essentially service centres were dependent upon the success of the wheat crop. The typical farmer was hardly a self-sufficient settler but rather a commercial producer, a small businessman, or, in Marxist terminology, an independent commodity producer and this determined a distinct set of interests and an agenda of political grievances. In the early years the farmers' associations were concerned with instituting a fair system of grading grain at the local elevators, with the provision of adequate transportation facilities and above all with low freight rates. The Canadian Pacific Railway came under intense criticism, not only for its early monopoly position, but also for a rate structure based on the principle of "fair discrimination" against those areas in which no water transport provided competition. Equally prominent in agrarian discontent was the agitation for less restrictive bank credit policies. Not only did loans extended through the banks carry a higher rate of interest in the west than elsewhere, but these were usually short-term commercial loans of three months which had to be repaid shortly after harvest. This inflexible rule, it was argued, compelled farmers to dispose off their crops all at once and thereby forced down the price. The issue of the tariff, however, came to displace all these inequities. The wheat farmer sold his product on the international market for a price determined by the competition of producers in Argentina, Australia and elsewhere. He purchased consumer goods and farm implements in a protected, domestic economy in which prices were artificially higher than they would be in conditions of competitive free trade. The Canadian farmers as a group could hardly affect the international price of wheat; what they could do was to increase their income through the reduction of the tariff which would lower their costs of production, and work towards the lowering of transport and credit costs. On some of these matters the federal government before the war proved to be sympathetic and responsive for its interests in securing the efficient operation of the wheat economy coincided with the farmers' complaints. Thus it established fairer standards in the grain trade and established freight rates for the export crops (in the Crow's Nest Pass agreement with the Canadian Pacific Railway) which, when they became fully operative, were one-fifth of the charges on comparable American routes. What the federal government could not do was alter the protective tariff for it was the lynchpin of its national economic policy and was resolutely defended by the industrial interests of Ontario and Quebec which were its main beneficiaries.

The system of economic policies was complemented by direct management from Ottawa and a very tight metropolitan control. Canada was to confront a resistance movement at Red River and a rebellion in the Northwest in 1885 as the result of assuming that the area was empty of people worth consulting but on the whole the extension of Canadian authority through the North-West Mounted Police and pacification of the demoralized native peoples through treaties was peaceful and orderly. As a result of the metis' resistance the miniscule province of Manitoba was created in 1870; with the growth of population the provinces of Saskatchewan and Alberta were established in 1905. These three new provinces, however, were quite unlike, the older provinces in the federation in that control over natural resources was reserved for the central government. This control was retained "for the purposes of the Dominion" not only because it was necessary for a coordinated land grant policy but also because Canada had resolved that the west was to pay for its own development. When the transcontinental railway was chartered it was given some 300,000 acres of land located throughout the fertile belt: the expectation was that as settlement and cultivation proceeded these lands would increase in value and that their sale would help defray the costs of building the railway, not only through the prairies, but on the barren wilderness north of the Great Lakes and through the mountains as well. The Canadian Pacific Railway had also been exempted from all forms of taxation in perpetuity: so little trust did the federal authorities have in the reliability of the prairie settlers that this exemption was written into the constitutions of the provinces of Alberta and Saskatchewan. In addition, of course, the federal government liberally employed its power of disallowing provincial legislation: over three-quarters of the provincial statutes disallowed before 1911 originated in the west (including British Columbia).

This degree of control was justified on the grounds that the Prairie West was a national estate, purchased by the people of old Canada, and therefore to be developed for the benefit of the nation as a whole. It was never intended that the west would remain in a position of political subordination forever, but on the other hand, there was no pre-set agenda for implementing local representative government. The territories outside Manitoba were at first governed by a Lieutenant Governor and nominated advisory council to which elected members were added as population increased. When this council became fully elective and attained responsible government it was prevented by federal authority from borrowing funds to build the material elements of a rapidly growing society and was dependent upon annual grants which never caught up with the real needs. Out of this financial predicament and dependency arose demands for provincial status but this was continually delayed for reasons of national party politics, and when implemented, provincial status was curtailed. The three western provinces in fact did not become provinces equal to the others in the Canadian federation until 1930 when control of resources was turned over to them. For some two generations their status resembled that of British North American colonies in the Empire in the early 19th century and the results were similar. The devolution of authority would have come in time in any case, but the fact that it was western politicians who agitated for provincial status, responsible government and control of resources made it seem that these had been extracted as a series of concessions from an obdurate federal government. And this experience imparted an anti-Ottawa bias to prairie politics which was to be augmented and consolidated in the future.

Prairie society and its regional character were also shaped in the formative period by the immigration policies of the federal government which encouraged the migration of experienced farmers virtually irrespective of their ethnic origins. In the fifteen years before the Great War some 2.5 million immigrants entered Canada from Britain, the United States and continental Europe; the population of the prairie region grew to 1.5 million in 1914.* By 1914 each of the prairie provinces contained substantial minorities of non-British, non-Canadian birth: these varied from 21 per cent in Manitoba, 33 per cent in Saskatchewan, to 38 per cent in Alberta. Not only was prairie society more ethnically diverse, than the older provinces but it also had a far higher proportion of people who had no experience of Canada and no sentimental attachment to its political and other institutions.

A good-deal–perhaps too much–has been made of this fact in weakening the ties between east and west and nurturing a regional sentiment. Some groups–especially pacifist sects like the Doukhobors, Mennonites and Hutterians–deliberately avoided any but the minimal economic relations with the surrounding society; others, like the more numerous Slavic peoples from eastern Europe, settled in cohesive blocs that were isolated from direct Anglo-

---

*In 1931 it was over 2 million, just under a quarter of Canada's total population.

Canadian influences, were preoccupied with the physical tasks of pioneering, and participated only passively in political life, usually supporting provincial parties sympathetic to their language rights in the school systems. When representatives of these people appeared in legislatures in the twenties they were invariably members of the national political parties. For all the suspicion directed at the republicanism of the Americans they actually blended easily into this frontier society: many of them were almost professional developers who worked and extended their homesteads into established farms, sold them at a profit, and moved on, not a few returning to the United States. As for the British, they were "preferred" immigrants but hardly privileged ones: the majority were urban people and many after trying their inexpert hands at farming (with results that still provide amusement on the prairies), gravitated to towns and cities. By transmitting ideas of democratic socialism the class conscious skilled workingmen exerted a profound impact upon the labour movement. The most significant group of all were the settlers and businessmen from Ontario who had preceded the great wave of foreign immigration and who before 1900 had established the basic institutional patterns and culture of the Prairie West. It is they who dominated for a long time the political elites, the farmers' associations, the Protestant denominations, boards of trade, the newspaper world, and the reform movements. And their influence was reinforced by the British and Americans who after all shared the foundations of their culture in a way the European foreigner did not.

The immigrants from eastern, central and southern Europe were accepted as economically indispensable but also as a threat to the maintenance of a British-Canadian culture. They were accused of being deficient in a sense of civic responsibility, unfamiliar with Canadian modes of government, and lacking in elementary standards of social behavior. The movement to assimilate, or "Canadianise" the foreigner drew support from many disparate sources, including simple prejudice against the unfamiliar, but its purpose—as well as the meaning of Canadianization—was spelled out by the Methodist Missionary Society in 1910: "Our objective on behalf of European foreigners should be to assist in making them English-speaking, Christian citizens who are clean, educated, and loyal to the Dominion and to Greater Britain." This was the ideal to be enforced above all through the educational systems and on this official level the movement was a success. This does not mean that immigrants were magically changed or that they or their descendents lost all knowledge of their own ancestral languages and cultures for they did not. It does however mean that the dominant culture was British-Canadian.

Not only did the fact of ethnic diversity intensify a resolve to assimilate the Europeans; it also strengthened a long-standing determination to eliminate what were regarded as the "special privileges" of French-Canadians. Whether or not the architects of confederation explicitly accepted the principle that the west was to become a joint possession of the two founding peoples of Canada is difficult to determine; the fact is, however, that constitutional guarantees were extended to official bilingualism in both Manitoba and the territories and to separate schools which meant in practice French language Catholic schools. In time these provisions of the federal government came to be seen as just as inappropriate to western conditions and aspirations as the instruments of political subordination. French-Canadians in the west were a tiny, vulnerable minority and were regarded as just another ethnic group; between the early 1890s and the late 1920s conflicts over schools and language ended in the elimination of bilingualism and biculturalism. Always the case was the same, the privileges of one small group could not be allowed to stand in the way of making the provincial school systems effective instruments of assimilation. This position was sustained by a potent anti-French, anti-Papist feeling but in the end the result was the same. The new western provinces had rejected the duality which was the foundation of accommodation in old Canada and had aligned itself with Ontario.

How closely the western provinces had become a new Ontario in attitude and culture was graphically illustrated in the Great War over the issue of conscription for overseas military service. The dominant groups in the west fully supported the necessity of conscription in order to guarantee not only allied victory but also Canada's claim to autonomy within the Empire, and in the election of 1917, the people of the three prairie provinces voted almost unanimously for the pro-conscriptionist coalition. Though this victory was ensured by extensive official manipulation of the electorate that neutralized the influence of European immigrants, and though westerners had only set aside, not forgotten, their disagreements with the central government, the outcome of 1917 election suggests the strength of the common nationalism and common culture that united them to the heartland of English Canada.

This union of opinion was quite transitory. Out of the intense social strains and class conflicts that erupted immediately after the war was born the Progressive Party which stands at the beginning of a tradition that became inseparable from western regionalism–the support for third-party protest movements. The classic two party system was disrupted in the war: the Liberals were little more than an anti-conscriptionist, highly protectionist Quebec rump; the unionist coalition had betrayed their promise not to conscript farmers' sons, had disappointed farmers by their wheat marketing policies, and above all were strongly committed to the tariff. The farmers who had previously forwarded their interests through the old parties clearly had nowhere to go except to enter the political arena as a separate force. Because of their numbers they easily captured the provincial governments of Alberta and Manitoba; in Saskatchewan the Liberals became an agrarian party in all but name. In the federal election of 1921 the Progressive party took 65 seats, including 37 of the 43 constituencies on the prairies. The party stood for a comprehensive reversal of the national policies which had underpinned Canadian economic development for half a century, and which, by artificially promoting industrialism and urbanization, had diminished the importance of the farmer in national life. Its platform proposed that the tariff be lowered and eventually eliminated to end the exploitation of the agricultural west by the east. In the demonology of the Progressives the "west" represented the people, the real producers of wealth, and the democratic promise; the "east" was equated with the interests of industry and financialism and the corrupt federal parties that served their purposes. The Progressive party was not only the expression of western regionalism (in fact 44 per cent of its popular vote came from the rural districts of Ontario) but also the rebellion of the farmers as a class. They did not challenge the values of commercial agriculture or capitalism in general: by calling for the nationalization of railways and the financial system the farmers were only advocating state intervention in support of *their* interests.

The Progressives were ineffectual in national politics because of internal divisions, a confusion over tactics, and the absorptive capacity of the Liberal party, and the movement faded away in the later twenties. It was of utmost significance, however, for sharpening and focusing regional discontent and for providing even by its failures lessons that were learned by two successor movements that appeared amid the devastation of the great depression which for the Prairie West brought a total collapse of the market for wheat, drought, destruction, and a crushing burden of debt. The Cooperative Commonwealth Federation was a social-democratic party that stood for nationalization, economic planning, and social security; the Social Credit Movement combined fundamentalist Christianity with an economic theory that attributed the depression to flaws in the financial system. Though both became national parties it was in the provinces that they were most successful, Social Credit becoming the government in Alberta in 1935, the C.C.F. in Saskatchewan in 1944. Despite essential differences in ideology, the practice of democracy and in social policy these parties were quite similar in two respects. Both accorded priority to protecting the security of farm ownership against foreclosure and the threats of eviction of their debt-ridden possessor. And both provided a channel through which provincial electorate could express their anger and bitterness at distant, oppressive forces in the east. For the C.C.F. the enemy was the corporate, monopoly capitalism; for Social Credit, the money power and the banks. When attempts by Social Credit to control the banks' operations in the provinces were disallowed by the federal government, this only reaffirmed the status of that party as protector of the peoples' rights.

This tradition of third party protest inaugurated by the Progressives and sustained by the C.C.F. and Social Credit became one of the most distinctive features of the political culture of the Prairie West. But it neither involved a total repudiation of national parties nor was it essentially a rejection of Canada. Only once in all the federal elections from 1921 to 1957 did the prairie electorate give less than 59 per cent of their vote to the two national parties. Western protest, moreover, has always aimed at integrating the region more closely into national life or at changing the rules of political economy to give greater justice to the people of the region. These three parties were never separatist. Ironically the protest tradition had itself served to further isolate the prairies from the national government.

Out of the trauma of the depression and the acceptance by the federal government of large social responsibilities after World War II, there emerged a clearer understanding of the national obligation to those parts of the country which had not benefited as much as others from national policies. The west was quite literally saved from bankruptcy only by the federal government. Through the Wheat Board the federal government committed itself to the sale of the whole wheat crop and to the stabilizations of prices. And it became a principle of national policy that citizens in all parts of the country must enjoy a minimum standard of social welfare and that the federal government must guarantee this to the poorer provinces through a system of equalization payments. In the west, these changes were translated into an unstated contract between region and the national government: the west accepted the protection of industry in the east, which it could not change in any case, in return for a strong central government that marketed the wheat crop, maintained low freight rates, and underwrote economic security.

Until the end of World War II the Prairie West could, with a minimum of over-simplification, be termed a region in the sense that economic and political attitudes transcended the provinces into which it was divided and separated it from the rest of Canada. Increasingly, however, several developments have drastically altered the basis of regionalism. Through extensive mechanization and the growth in average farm size, fewer and fewer farmers produced ever larger yields. By 1971 the farm population constituted only 17 per cent of the population of the three provinces. Wheat is still of great importance, particularly in Saskatchewan, but the west remains a unique agricultural society only in selective historical memory. With the development of new resources and urbanization, westerners have become in social character and outlook much like other Canadians or North Americans. These changes have undermined that combination of agrarian grievance and regional identity which characterized protest politics in the past. Estrangement from the federal government persisted and grew in intensity during the 1970s but it fed on new issues and was expressed through national political parties rather than a regional protest party. How the Conservative party—once identified as the party of protection—came to dominate the prairies is a complex story. It has a good deal to do with the leader of that party and Prime Minister during the late fifties who took very seriously the national obligations to the agricultural constituency; it has much to do also with the preoccupation of Liberal governments with reaching some accommodation with the quiet revolution in Quebec since 1960. That preoccupation led to the promotion of official bilingualism and biculturalism and to making the national government and its institutions a reflection of the basic ethnic duality of Canada. These policies were greeted with hostility in a region which had always prized individual over group rights and which had long ago settled matters of ethnic rights. The consequence of this and other policies was the virtual extinction of the Liberal party on the prairies. The point, however, is that dissatisfaction with the government party has been expressed through two parties–the Conservative and to a lesser extent the New Democratic Party (a moderate successor to the C.C.F.)–which are national, not regional.

Perhaps the most crucial change of the last generation that has affected all Canada as well as the west is the growth in power and prestige of provincial governments relative to the central government. The growth in those functions of the state which fall under provincial jurisdiction in education, highway construction, welfare and health care have not only enhanced provincial power but have generated large and active bureaucracies. Through their control of natural resources, the provinces have been the chief beneficaries of the exploitation of petroleum, natural gas, potash, minerals, and timber. The governments of Alberta, and to a lesser degree Saskatchewan, are no longer content to simply take their share of royalties; they are pursuing strategies that will diversify their economies, end the dependence upon the export of raw resources, and create industries and jobs–based on the local resources. What they are proposing to do for the western provinces is what Ontario and Quebec accomplished long ago with hydroelectricity, minerals, and timber. In the case of oil-rich Alberta, however, this strategy has encountered large obstacles, some of its own making, some the result of national policies. Economic diversification is inhibited by the very freight structure which farmers in the past had fought for–rates that favor the export of raw resources and are much higher on manufactured goods. Attempts to modify these rates have encountered political opposition not only from wheat farmers within the province of Alberta but also from Saskatchewan which is far more dependent on agriculture than its neighbor. But the main obstacle has been the federal government. Throughout the seventies the Conservative provincial government of Alberta was locked in continual conflict with the Liberal government at Ottawa over energy policy, regulation of exports, and pricing of oil. When the federal government set the domestic price of oil below the world level those with long memories recalled that during the Great War Ottawa froze the price of wheat sold to the Allies below the international level. Why the federal government regulated the price of oil and wheat and not the resources found in other, more electorally powerful, jurisdictions needed little explanation. The population of Ontario is greater than that of the three prairie provinces combined and those provinces have, relative to the representation of the other more populous provinces, fewer members in the House of Commons than they had in 1930. The effectiveness of Prairie representatives was hardly increased since virtually all of them sat on the opposition benches. The case for the federal government's oil pricing policies was difficult to make in the west: it was not made any easier by the fact that a federal Crown Corporation at the same time insistently resisted any other role for western oil than as a feeder to the petrochemical industry in southern Ontario.

Regionalism has been provincialized in Alberta which contains half the prairie population and is one of the richest provinces in Canada. Just as successive politicians in Quebec have claimed to speak for the French Canadian nation, so too the Alberta Premier has associated his causes with the old agrarian struggles against central Canada, and has frequently reminded his supporters that the federal government controlled western resources for sixty years and is showing itself interested in doing so again. The essential case is that the west has paid excessively for national unity in the past and should now be freed from national policy constraints to correct this injustice. (It is not rewarding for a political economist to point out that the lack of secondary industry in the west is due as much, if not more, to distance from markets and a small population than to any national policies.) Regional sentiment is not only reflected by politicians, it is partly created by them. The tensions inherent in a federal system have presented irresistible opportunities to exploit differences for partisan ends: the Conservative Premier of Alberta recently appealed to the electorate to give him a strong hand in the difficult, upcoming negotiations with Ottawa over oil prices. Regionalism is further exaggerated by regular federal-provincial diplomatic gatherings when an advantage is to be gained by extreme opening statements for the benefit of the folks back home; unless one is interested in a career in federal politics (which few premiers entertain). The system of election by majority vote in single-member constituencies sustains a distorted impression of unanimity: oven in inhospitable Alberta the Liberal party has taken up to 30 per cent of the popular vote but no seats.

Regionalism as a sense of psychological separateness is not a static quality but a tendency that has varied in intensity over time and has changed in character over the last thirty years. Prairie regionalism arose out of the geographical isolation of the area from the rest of Canada, an agricultural economy, and the subordinate relationship of that economy to the national policy. It is possible to write the history of the west as little more than a series of unsuccessful revolts against central authority and the dominance of central Canada, but to do so would miss a very essential element of that history–the strong ties of culture and sentiment that linked the west to the rest of the country, especially to Ontario. One need only mention the common nationalism of the two world wars, the numerous nation-wide associations, common religious institutions, and the Canadian Broadcasting Corporation to suggest the importance of these links. This English Canadian culture has offset and contained the differences arising from economic interests. The result was to give Prairie regionalism a peculiar thrust–it is profoundly federalist in the sense of seeking equitable treatment and also changing its status from that of a junior partner to one of equality. At bottom westerners have always been concerned with making the national government–too often seen as the government of someone else–their government. (This is a very different position from the separatist strand in French-Canadian nationalism.) One of the enduring obstacles to the realization of this maturity has been the disparity in numbers. Not a little of the frustration evident in Alberta in recent years arises from the combination of great potential power combined with political impotence. Highly imaginative suggestions for altering the moribund Senate to reflect provincial or regional viewpoints, or making appointments of more westerners to federal government agencies and regulatory bodies will hardly solve the problem for it is at bottom a question of how to accord representation to a region relatively small in population in a state based on the rule of the majority.

5

EDUCATION AND COMMUNALISM IN INDIA : 1870-1947

Aparna Basu

Communalism in India is too complex a process to be explained in terms of any single determinant. The roots of the separatist movement leading to the partition of India are diverse and tortuous. The British Raj came to an end amidst enormous convulsions in which millions of Hindus, Muslims, and Sikhs were killed and large populations were shunted across new frontiers. Events of such magnitude have led historians to seek explanations of equal significance. Among the causal explanations offered, the most widely accepted one, in the pre-Independence period, among the nationalists, was the British policy of divide and rule. The presence of an outside power, eager to promote and exacerbate communal divisions was a critical factor.[1] A number of scholars–Pakistani and Indians–have put forward the thesis that the Hindus and Muslims were always two nations.[2] Hindu-Muslim interaction has been characterised as "a clash of two civilizations, of two peoples who had different languages, different literary roots, different ideas of education, different philosophical sources . . . such a yawning cultural gulf was enough to destroy any affinity which the two people might have had and to bring to nought all efforts at unity."[3] The social and religious difference between the two communities, it is said, was "so acute and fundamental, that even seven hundred years of close residence failed to make the least crack in it."[4] The economic backwardness of Muslims and the delayed emergence of a middle class among them is popular as an explanation among scholars influenced by Marxist sociology.[5] It has often been argued that the economic problem was fundamental, but the exploiting classes misled the masses and channelled their frustrations into communal forms of expression.[6] "Religion was brought in primarily because it could be utilised to 'mask' the politics of classes and social groups arising in the secular, non-religions spheres.[7] If leftist historiography has emphasized material interests and economic forces, there are a number of others who equate communalism with communal politics. The conflict, it is argued was not between communities but between the competing elites of different communities.[8] A number of historians have concentrated on the constitutional system and its influence in determining communal politics.[9] Democratic politics, with its emphasis on numbers, was likely to lead to communal polarisation in a society fragmented into antagonistic religious communities. The nationalist movement is accused of using religious idioms and symbols thus importing communal overtones into the movement itself, instead of developing a revolutionary, secular ideology.[10] The leadership of Tilak, Aurobindo, Lajpat Rai and others became identified with Hindu revivalism.[11] The strategy adopted by the Indian National Congress has been held responsible for separation.[12] It has been urged by some that Islam with its rigid and fanatical ethos, was bound to promote separatist politics, and by others that Hinduism with its caste system did not have the institutional openness needed for the construction of a composite nation. Religion was an important force in the evolution of modern India, a factor which has been often neglected both by left-wing as well as liberal historians.[13]

India consisted of communities at different stages of social, economic and political development advancing at different rates; the gaps which thus developed explain the particular shape and evolution of communal politics. The Muslims were, in particular, a backward community and hence compelled to pursue their communal interests exclusively.[14] Beyond this, some attention has been given to the role of historical writing in fanning the flames of communalism.[15]

Education was only one distinct component among the various forces which contributed to the growth of communalism in India but it is of sufficient importance to merit separate consideration. In this paper we shall examine government education policy and how far it contributed to the growth of communal consciousness, as well as analyse developments in education and their impact on communal politics with particular reference to Bengal–a Muslim majority province where Muslims were educationally backward and the United Provinces, a Muslim minority province where Muslims were educationally advanced.

English education in the 19th century was not merely a means to acquire knowledge or to develop one's moral and intellectual faculties. It was the key to government employment and a passport to the new professions. The growth of education was not, however, uniform throughout the whole country. It varied from province to province and within a province among different castes, communities and linguistic groups. The earliest beneficiaries of the system were mostly the high caste Hindus who had a tradition of literacy and who recognised the national advantages that it offered and flocked to the new institutions eager to grasp the opportunities opened up by colonial rule. In Bengal, where English education first began, the Muslims lagged far behind. The movement for western education, among them, started fairly late in the 19th century. By then a sizeable English educated Hindu *bhadralok* class had already emerged. Hence the anxiety of the Muslim elite and their efforts to extract concessions from the government to counter-balance the advantages gained by the Hindus.

Throughout the 19th century attempts were made to analyze the causes of Muslim backwardness and diagnose in particular the problems of their education. It was commonly accepted that the Muslims, less nimble than the Hindus, were less ready to seize the opportunities offered by Western education and less quick to adapt themselves to changing conditions under British rule. While the Hindus were crowding schools and colleges, the Muslims sat apart, wrapped in the memory of their traditions and held back by the conservatism of Islam. Hunter blamed the education system for the condition of the Muslims:

> The truth is that our system of public instruction which has awakened the Hindus from the sleep of centuries and quickened their inert masses . . . is opposed to the traditions, unsuited to the requirements, and hateful to the religion of the Musalmans.[16]

Rev. Long argued that Muslims did not have the same aptitude as the Hindus for acquiring a knowledge of English. He compared this with the Irish situation where the English had decided "that no Irishman should hold office unless he knew English" a mistake from which England was now suffering." He hoped that the English would not commit the same mistake in India.[17]

Bengal was a classic case of Muslim backwardness in education.

In 1874-5, in Bengal proper, while, Muslims formed 48.8 per cent of the population but, only 29 per cent of pupils in schools were Muslims . . . Hindus formed 50.1 per cent of the population but 70.1 per cent of school pupils were Hindus.[18] The higher the level of education, rarer were the Muslims. In 1875, of the total number of college students, 5.4 per cent were Muslims and 93.9 per cent were Hindus.[19] Why did the Muslims lag behind in education? During the first few years of the East India Company's rule, the Muslim aristocracy had retained its hold over government offices–revenue, judicial and executive. The administrative reforms of Lord Cornwallis dealt the first major blow to this monopoly, since, under the new system, all higher posts were reserved for Englishmen. The Muslim *amils* and *faujdars* lost their administrative pre-eminence with the appointment of English Collectors in the districts. The Permanent Settlement (1793) and the Resumption proceedings deprived many Muslim landed families of their livelihood. There were not many opportunities for rising up in the army and military service under the company attracted few; the Muslims soldiery was virtually superseded by the newly recruited sepoys. For the Muslim elite in Bengal, British conquest meant the destruction of a way of life as well as of sources of income which would have enabled them to take advantage of higher education.

Those who could afford to send their children to schools were often reluctant to do so because they regarded the new learning as un-Islamic and were afraid of conversion to Christianity. Others regarded traditional Islamic learning as infinitely superior and basked in the memories of their past glories. While Hindu boys went to Hindu College (established in 1817) and acquired western learning, Muslims went to the Calcutta Madrasa (founded by Warren Hastings in 1782) which gave them traditional Islamic learning placing considerable emphasis on Muhammedan law and jurisprudence. If they overcame the problem of finance, pride and prejudice, there was still the problem of language.

Most Muslims felt obliged to acquire some basic knowledge of the 'Islamic languages'–i.e., Arabic, Persian and Urdu, in addition to Bengali and English. Learning five languages often proved too much of a strain.

Economic decline, religious prejudice, the language problem were all there, but do not explain the poor showing of Muslims in higher education in Bengal, for how then can we account for the fact that in the North Western Provinces and Oudh, where the Muslims were in a minority, they not only held their own in education but were holding a share much in excess of their population.[20] Unlike Bengal, in U.P. the Muslims were mainly an urbanized,[21] non-agricultural[22] and professional community.[23] In East Bengal, on the other hand, the majority of Muslims were low-caste Hindu converts and there was little difference between their position in respect of education and that of Namasudras or Rajbansis–low caste Hindus with whom they were ethnically and occupationally allied. Just as poor Hindu peasants could not afford education, neither could poor Muslims.[24] It is misleading to compare Hindus and Muslims as monolithic units. There were extreme variations in literacy and education among different castes. As higher caste Hindus were much more advanced educationally,[25] so also upper class Muslims were ahead of lower class converted Muslims, such as Julahas, Kulus, Nais or Bhisthis. The position of Syeds among Muslims was comparable to that of Brahmins among Hindus. This was true not only of Bengal but also of U.P.[26]

Muslims lagged behind in education not only because of pride of race, religious fear, linguistic difficulties and memories of bygone superiority, but also because in the predominantly Muslim majority areas of East Bengal, West Punjab and Sind, they were peasant to whom education was neither useful nor necessary. Education in the rural areas was in a very backward state. British policy had been to concentrate on the urban areas. In those provinces where Muslims were engaged in trade and commerce, as in Bombay, or in the professions, as in U.P., they were not so much behind at least at the primary and secondary level and in U.P. not even at the University stage.[27] The influence of occupation on education is evident from the fact that while literacy was widespread among the trading and business castes, they did not go in for higher education. The Bengal model was, however, applied to the rest of India and a policy was adopted which suited the British as well as a section of the Muslim elite.

Around the 1870s there was a change in the attitude of the government towards Indian Muslims with Wahabi trials of 1870-71 which had revealed a section of the community's profound disaffection. It was realised that it may not be politically wise to keep a community so sullen, specially when there were signs that educated Hindus were becoming critical of British rule. There were a number of high government officials who since 1857 were ready to believe in a general Muslim conspiracy, but there were others who were arguing against condemning the whole community. "The existence side by side of these hostile creeds," wrote Strachey, "is one of the strong points in our political position in India. The better class of Mohammedans are a source of strength and not of weakness to us. They constitute a comparatively small but energetic minority of the population whose political interests are identical with ours."[28] There was a feeling among these officials that unless effective measures were adopted to reconcile Muslims to British rule, they might pose a serious threat to the Raj. Lord Mayo asked W.W. Hunter, a Bengal Civilian, to write a book on 'Are Indian Musalmans bound by their religion to rebel against the Queen?' The question posed in the title assumed an identity based on religion, but Hunter also refers to Muslims as a 'class,' a 'community', a 'people,' a 'nationality,' and a 'race'. Hunter opens the book by saying that "The whole Muhammedan community has been openly deliberating on their obligation to rebel." The danger to British rule comes from "the fanatical masses," efforts must be made by the British to win over "well-to-do Musalmans" who do not take their religion so seriously. He made a strong plea for a policy of reconciliation. In the same year, Mayo wrote a note suggesting the means to persuade Muslims to enter government schools and colleges more willingly and to revive the Calcutta Madrasa. This led to the issuing a Government of India Resolution on 7 August 1871, drawing special attention to the problems of Muslim education.

In his *Indian Musalmans* published in 1871, Hunter pleaded for the establishment of special educational facilities for Muslims in order to win them over. He suggested various ways by which government could assist Muslim education–by establishing separate schools, by appointing Muslim teachers in existing schools and by appointing Muslim inspectors. The Education Commission (1882-84) made 17 recommendations regarding special provisions for Muslim education and the Government of India Resolution of 1884 suggesting that the problem of Muslim education be given "separate consideration" showed the working of the minds of officials.

British efforts aimed at encouraging Muslim education initiated in 1870-71 continued till 1947. The relevant measures followed two broad patterns. First, the government tried to make the ordinary secular schools attractive to the Muslims by giving scholarships to Muslim pupils in schools and training colleges; including Arabic, Persian and Urdu in the curriculum; providing hostels for Muslim boys and appointing Muslim educational officers and teachers. Secondly, measures were taken to improve madrasas and maktabs, bring them under the supervision of the Education Departments and introduce secular instruction. A few instances will suffice. After the partition of Bengal in 1905 in the new province of East Bengal and Assam, reserved scholarships were established for Muslims all the way from primary schools to the University stage. Provisions were made for the extended employment of Muslims in the education service.[29] In Madras and Bombay measures were introduced which allowed Muslim boys in government schools to pay only half the ordinary fees, and in some cases, no fees at all. Similar concessions were given everywhere.

With the reversal of the partition of Bengal in 1912, the Government of India felt that some special measures ought to be taken regarding the education of Muslims. The Government of Bengal appointed a special committee to consider the question connected with Muhammedan Education, under the chairmanship of Hornell, the D.P.I. The Committee's main recommendations were accepted by the Bengal government and soon implemented. Elementary Urdu books dealing with subject of special interests to Muslims were introduced in schools. Seats were reserved for Muslims in all government schools and colleges and work here was suspended for one hour on Fridays to enable Muslim boys to perform *jumma* prayers. Every effort was made to stress the separateness of Muslims in educational institutions by offering them special places, scholarships, hostels, books, teachers, to the extent of stressing the importance of Muslim dress and cap.

Unlike Bengal, in U.P., far from being backward, the Muslim elite constituted a dominant group bent upon proving its dominance and preventing the rise of self-assertion of the Hindus and the achievement by the Hindus of a share proportionate to their numbers in education and government service. Separatism here was the ideology of the dominant upper class Muslim elite anxious to retain if not its dominance, at least equality with the Hindus.

In U.P. the vernacular used as an official language, together with English, was Urdu in the Persian script. Between 1868 and 1900, Hindus began agitating for the replacement of Urdu by Hindi. The controversy between Hindi and Urdu became one of the most divisive issues between Hindus and Muslims.

The Hindi movement had its origin among educated Hindus in Benaras in the 1860s. In 1882, the supporters of Hindi submitted to the Education Commission 118 memorials from cities and towns all over the province and signed by some 67,000 persons.[30] The main line of argument used was that the use of Urdu in schools was retarding the progress of primary education.[31] Behind the dispute between the supporters of Hindi in the Devnagri script and Urdu in the Persian script, there lay a cleavage between the aspirations and interests of educated Hindus and Muslims. Both the movements were led by educated members of each community and they fostered both linguistic and cultural divergences between them. Throughout this period, education in the United Provinces became a political issue of great importance and was influenced by the competing aspirations of the politico-literary elites. In the process, language and education, which once united elite segments of Hindu and Muslims, came to be used for purposes of competitive mobilisation between elite Hindus and elite Muslims, offering to the rural masses alternative standards for the same language and reinforcing religious division thereby.

These divisions also took organisational form through the development of voluntary associations promoting the spread of Hindu and Urdu. The leading organisation of the Hindi movement in the late 19th century was the Nagari Pracharini Sabha, formed in Benaras in 1893. In 1910, the Hindi Sahitya Sammelan was formed in Allahabad. On the Urdu side, the Anjuman Taraqqi-e-Urdu was formed in 1903 and has remained the leading Urdu voluntary association in north India ever since. These Hindi and Urdu associations through their activities, and through their close connections with prominent political leaders and organisations in U.P. including the Congress, the Aligarh movement and the Muslim League, contributed to the growth of separatist sentiment among Hindus and Muslims alike. Sir Syed Ahmed and his followers played a key role in defending Urdu during this period.

It has been argued that the Hindi-Urdu controversy of the late 19th century was the critical factor in the development of Muslim separatism and was responsible for a change in the attitude of U.P. Muslims towards the Congress. Some historians and political scientists have challenged this view and argue that religion was the overriding criterion in Syed Ahmed's conception of nationality, not language.[33] Paul Brass holds the view that elite groups of Hindus and Muslims used the symbols of language and religion in their competition for jobs and political power. "Religion and language were the symbolic instruments in this essentially political conflict."[34]

It was not only the British government which supported denominational educational institutions. A large number of Hindus and Muslims were also anxious to devise separate systems of education for themselves. Nawab Abdul Latif recommended the establishment of separate primary schools for lower class Muslims.[35] Syed Ameer Ali, himself a London trained barrister, was equally opposed to any mixed schools and colleges and suggested that maktabs and madrasas attached to mosques should be utilized for segregated education.[36]

Sir Syed Ahmed Khan established the Muhammedan Anglo Oriental College in Aligarh in 1877. The circular issued by the College Fund Committee set out the institution's origins and aims: "Ever since the fall of the Mogul Empire . . . the Musalmans have steadily been losing ground . . . of late the English language having become an indispensable requirement for any office under the government, the Musalmans have most remarkably fallen off the list of government appointments." Nothing but education could "remedy the evils from which they are now suffering." But because the government's education system was "not suited to the domestic and social requirements" of the Muslims, few of them went to these schools, therefore, it had been decided by leading Muslims to start a college on the pattern of Oxford and Cambridge, which it was hoped would "attract the higher classes of the Muhammedans." The curriculum was a compromise between Muslim education and Western learning. The college was to teach English, Western Science as well as Urdu, Persian, Arabic and the tenets of Islam.

Sir Syed envisaged a college, where "like the churches of Oxford and Cambridge, there will be mosques attached to each college. . . . It will be mandatory for boys in residence to join the congregational prayers (*namaz*) at all the five times." Muslim students were to have separate uniforms.

The founders of Aligarh spoke in the name of all Muslims but offered a programme designed to make contact with only the north Indian Muslims literate in Urdu. The high tuition fees and its residential character ensured that M.A.O. College would provide education primarily to the aristocratic and upper class of Muslims.[38]

The M.A.O. College was a profoundly political enterprise. Education at Aligarh was meant to develop cordial relations between the Muslims and the English in India. Hence in the early years the Principal and staff were all recruited from England. In addition, Sir Syed wanted to train here a class of future leaders for the entire Muhammedan community in India. He desired that Aligarh should impart to its students an Islamic identity and a sense of Muslim solidarity.[39]

In 1886, Sir Syed Ahmed Khan founded the Muhammedan Education Conference to promote the educational objectives of the M.A.O. College and extend its influence throughout India. He wanted Muslims everywhere to concentrate their efforts on Aligarh so that a network of Muslim institutions in India should emerge. The Conference, however, took up political issues and became the Muslim counterpart to the Congress till the foundation of the Muslim League in 1906. Throughout these years Aligarh was the centre of Muslim educational and political activity.

The idea of a Muslim University at Aligarh was not new. It was first put forward after Sir Syed's death in 1899. But the scheme did not materialise and it was only in 1911 that the Aga Khan and the Muslim University Foundation Committee officially approached Harcourt Butler, the Education Member. When the scheme was referred to London, it received strong support from Theodore Morison, a former principal of the M.A.O. College, who was at that time member of the India Council. Morison's thesis was that Muslims were a nationality, not a sect, and it was not quite correct to use the word denominational in connection with Aligarh University. Islam and Hinduism stood for totally different conceptions of life, no common will or common interests united Hindus and Muslims, and it was not really possible to educate two such entirely different communities together. Morison, therefore, thought it impolitic, in the highest degree, to oppose communal universities, since "Spontaneous organisations of the people even when claiming to be *national* have all been upon the old lines of separate communities. The nationalism of which we hear most and which professes to be all-Indian is really Hindu nationalism."[40] Morison was supported in the India Council by Baig, James La Touche and William Lee Warner and therefore in spite of Morley's apprehensions about denominational Universities, London gave a green signal to Delhi to proceed in their negotiations with the Muslims for a university at Aligarh.[41] From the strictly educational point of view there seemed little justification for a Muslim University; "the demand was a political battlecry" but "to apply a new university as a remedy to the existing backward condition of Mohammedan education would be like a prescription of a pill for a sprained elbow." Sir John Hewitt, Lieutenant-Governor of U.P., opposed the idea on the ground that denominational universities would add to the already existing communal tensions in his province, but his government finally decided to support the scheme for political reasons.[42] Neither Lord Hardinge, nor his Council approved of denominational universities. The Finance Member thought that not a penny of government money should go to a Hindu or Muslim University.[43] Yet the Viceroy approved of the scheme because it would be "extremely dangerous to discourage this Muslim undertaking and would be unwise to show hostility to the idea since "we should have the whole of the Musalmans of India against us."[44]

Communal considerations were continually influencing the formulation of education policy. The scheme for a University at Dacca originated with Lord Hardinge's visit to the city, shortly after the reversal of the partition of Bengal. Replying to an address presented to him in Dacca on 31 December 1911, the Viceroy said that education was the true salvation of the Muslims and the Government of India would recommend a University at Dacca.[45] The Calcutta University Commission also strongly supported a University at Dacca and suggested the establishment of a department of Islamic studies and special halls of residence for Muslim students.[46] Though not visualised as a denominational university, it was expected, that because of its location, it would help the cause of education of the Muslims of Bengal. What Aligarh did for the Muslim separatist movement in the subcontinent as a whole, Dacca did for it in East Bengal. The majority of its students and teachers until 1947 were Hindus, but an increasing number of Muslim students were being educated here. The University supplied the Muslim League with a large body of students and teachers drawn from different parts of East Bengal to work for it. In the Bengal Legislative Assembly after 1935, most of the Muslim members elected from East Bengal had been educated at Dacca. The Dacca university thus helped to create a politically conscious, educated Muslim middle class in East Bengal.

While the Universities of Aligarh and Dacca created an English educated Muslim elite, there were Muslims who still feared that Islamic religion and culture were being threatened by the British educational system. The most vital school of traditional learning in the second half of the 19th century was at Deoband, the *dar-al-ulum* founded in 1867 by Muhammad Qasim Nanotawi and Rashid Ahmed Gangohi.[47] The course of study was strictly traditional–Arabic, prosody, rhetoric, grammar, logic, *fiqh, tafsir, tibb* (medicine) and a little philosophy. The medium of instruction was Urdu; no English was taught and no modern science. Deoband devoted itself principally to the conservation of the theological learning, in general, and certain elements of the school of Waliullah in particular. As a theological seminary of repute it attracted scholars from all over India.

The graduates of Deoband taught in madrasas and maktabs of Muslim India, became preachers, printers and book binders. Firangi Mahal and Nadwat-al-ulama at Lucknow imparted a similar kind of tradiional learning.[48] Shibli declared the purpose of Nadwat to defend Islam against "contemporary times." Supposed to maintain middle line between Aligarh and Deoband, its products were indistinguishable from those of Deoband in theological and intellectual outlook. Curiously the separatist movement which was ostensibly based on an appeal to the religious sentiments of the Muslims, found little favour among the ulama of Deoband and Firangi Mahal who opposed the modernist tendencies of Aligarh. The number of ulama in U.P. was small, in 1921, only around 10,000 Muslims made their living by religion, their influence was, therefore, limited. U.P., unlike Bengal, also had a sizeable Muslim professional middle class. The ulema, men like Abdul Bari and others actively supported the Khilafat movement. While they supported the freedom movement, the ulama also thought in terms of an Islamic identity. The goal of Deoband was to maintain religious identity of Muslims.

Just as there was a demand for separate institutions for Muslims, so also the Hindus wanted universities and schools of their own. The movement for the foundation of Benares Hindu University was closely linked with that of the Aligarh Muslim University. The scheme formulated by Pandit Madan Mohan Malaviya envisaged the establishment of a university for the promotion of Sanskrit learning and proposed Hindi as the medium of instruction. The object of the

University was "to promote the study of the Hindu Shastras and of Sanskrit literature generally as a means of preserving and popularizing for the benefit of the Hindus in particular and of the world at large in general, the best thought and culture of the Hindus, and all that was good and great in the ancient civilization of India. "At the same time it wanted to advance and diffuse . . . scientific, technical and professional knowledge." Malaviya conceived of a University which would revive the best traditions of the ancient Gurukulas and combine with them the best of the modern universities of the West. The University as it finally emerged as a result of the efforts of Malaviya, Annie Besant and the Maharaja of Darbhanga aimed at combining spirituality with science, modern learning with Hindu philosophy.

The Gurukul at Kangri, near Hardwar, started by Munshiram in 1907 was a modern version of the schools of learning in ancient India. The emphasis was on the Vedic studies and the medium was Hindi. The institution formulated its own syllabus and had its own text books. Shabil's Saras-Mir was inspired by the Gurakul, If Deoband produced maulvis, the Gurukulas trained Arya Samaj preachers. Such denominational institutions contributed to the growth of a feeling of rivalry between the different communities in India.

Expanding facilities for education led to a steady increase in the number of educated. In 1917, there were over 7 million pupils in schools and colleges, by 1937 the number had doubled.[51] There were about 4,000 graduates in 1917 and nearly 20,000 in 1937. The total number of Muslim pupils was growing faster than the school population of other communities. Taking British India as a whole, in the decade 1912-27, the number of Muslim pupils in educational institutions recognised by the government increased from one and a half million to two and a half million.[52] Muslims were attending schools in larger numbers in proportion to their population, than pupils of all other communities put together. This improvement in the absolute numbers of educated Muslims tended to come from those classes enfranchised by the 1919 Reforms and directly interested in the material advantages.

This educational expansion in the 1920s was not matched by enlarged economic opportunities. In the years after the First World War there was a decline in the level of both agricultural and industrial production, and an overall decline in both expenditure on goods and services in the public sector.[53] Cuts in public expenditure meant fewer roads, buildings or irrigation contracts, fewer government jobs and teaching posts relative to the increased numbers of those qualified to hold them. There was a growing rivalry among the educated classes for the scarce loaves and fishes, which was reflected in the increasing communal bitterness in the legislature and at the local level in municipal boards. Serious communal riots occurred in India between 1922 and 1927.[54] The hatred and violence of the streets may have been held in check had the resentment of schools, colleges, offices and shops not been sharpened by the disappointment and frustration of the educated classes. India was prey in the inter-war years, to the tensions generated among the middle classes, who found that a stagnant economy was thwarting their rising expectations.

In the Hindu majority provinces, the Muslim minority blamed the Hindus for depriving them of jobs and opportunities, and in the Muslim majority provinces it was just the reverse. The *Shuddhi* and *Sangathan* movements among the Hindus, the *Tabligh* and *Tanzim* movements among the Muslims were constant reminders that Hindus were Hindus and Muslims were Muslims.

The Montague-Chelmsford Reforms helped to sharpen communal awareness by retaining separate electorates. Under "dyarchy", education became a transferred subject under an Indian Minister responsible to the provincial legislature which had an elected majority. Such responsibility offered political patronage which was often preferentially dispensed to members of the Minister's own caste or community.

Fazlul Haq became Minister of Education in Bengal under dyarchy and initiated a programme of educational expansion likely to benefit Muslims. Government grants were sanctioned for an Islamia College in Calcutta which was started in 1926. Both he and Abdur Rahim, Executive Councillor, pressed for more government aid for madrasas and maktabs, and there was considerable increase in the number of such institutions and their enrollment after 1922. The number of pupils in the higher madrasas doubled between 1922 and 1927 from 25,036 to 50,999.[55] The number of maktabs also increased by half and the number of pupils by more than half.[56] By 1927, Bengal had the largest number of maktabs.[57] It was generally the rural *ashraf* who preferred a religious oriented education to a secular one and sent their children to madrasas and maktabs.

The special institutions for Muslims in Bengal fell into five categories. There were Islamic Intermediate Colleges in Dacca, Chittagong and Serajganj. The first two were government run and the third became an aided institution after 1923. They taught *fiqh*, *hadis*, *Quran*, *Kalima*, logic and Islamic history. Madrasas were of two types–high and middle, corresponding to high and middle English Schools. They taught Urdu and Arabic. The junior madrassahs, where, in addition Bengali and English were taught became very popular in Bengal. In maktabs the rudiments of Islamic theology and law were imparted. In some schools, recitation of the Quran and Islamic ritual in simple Urdu were the main subjects. Lastly, there were schools for training maktab teachers.

Muslim revivalist movements, seeking reasons for the decline of Muslim power in India and elsewhere, found the explanation in the decline of Islamic religion and ideology from the pristine purity of Islam in its formative period. A return to these original practices of Islam naturally meant eliminating all heretical ceremonies and rituals derived from Hindu-Muslim religious interaction. Similarly, Hindu reformist and revivalist movements stressed Hindu symbols and a "return to the Vedas". The need for religious reform induced an intensive campaign of Islamization in Bengal in the latter part of the 19th century. Efforts of the mullahs and preachers to popularize the symbols and slogans of Islam came to be linked to a larger political goal, euphemistically described as Islamic solidarity, which envisaged the unity of all Muslims and their separation from all others, particularly Hindus. These campaigns of Islamization owed their success partially to the *anjumans* which in turn were often organized by the graduates of madrasas, scores of whom were now passing out regularly. The madrasa-educated scholars often found themselves employed as teachers in maktabs and junior madrasas, as maulvis, munshis, kazis or as Imams in mosques, teaching the rural children the rudiments of Islam. The spread of religious education had a direct bearing on the Islamization of the rural masses; not only were religious teachers more numerous, they now had a better knowledge of the principles of Islam and were well equipped to present these more effectively to their lay audiences. As literacy spread in the rural areas in Bengal, more and more Muslims could read cheap popular religious books, commonly known as the *naishat namahs* whose purpose was to Islamize the Muslim masses.[58] They rejected all customs and practices alien to Islam, however integral they might be to the life of rural Muslims. These theological tracts started circulating from the later 19th century. Besides condemning un-Islamic beliefs and practices, these *naishat namahs*, emphasized the importance of a truly pious life, interpreted as a life based on the strict observance of the essential practice of Islam. *Namaz*, or ritual prayer, for instance, was given extreme importance.

Apart from aiding maktabs and madrasas, the Bengal government also took measures to encourage the entry of Muslims into the ordinary educational institutions. In Chittagong College, the percentage of seats reserved for Muslims was raised from 25 to 30 per cent. One-fourth of the seats in the Bengal Engineering College and in the Ashanullah School of Engineering at Dacca were reserved for Muslims from 1925 onwards.[59] Many secondary schools were meant wholly or mainly for Muslims.[60] A certain percentage of seats in all aided and government schools was reserved for Muslims. Scholarships, stipends and freeships were bestowed on them liberally. Special inspecting officers, masters and maulvis were appointed in aided and government schools. Special hostels were opened for Muslim boys and Dacca University had a special Muslim hall of residence. In 1925-26, the government laid down rules regulating the proportion of Muslims in the Bengal education department.[61]

A study of government grants reveals that these were lavishly sanctioned to madrasas and maktabs. In 1938, government sanctioned a sum of Rs. 50,000 for purchase of land for a college for Muslim girls; eventually Lady Brabourne College, originally meant for Muslim girls, was established in Park Circus, a predominantly Muslim area of Calcutta.

As a result of all these efforts the number of Muslim pupils in Bengal doubled between 1922 and 1937. In 1921-22, the ratio of Muslim pupils to the Muslim population was 3.5 per cent; but in 1937 it was 6.0 per cent.[62]

The Government of India Act of 1919 increased the number of Muslim voters in Bengal from 6,346 to 465,127. The government was anxious to spread education among the enfranchised population and the Bengal (Rural) Primary Education Bill was introduced in the Legislative Council in August 1930. It recommended an education cess, the burden of which was to be largely borne by the landlords, most of whom were Hindus. In the Legislative Council, the Hindu members urged that the Bill be referred to a Select Committee while the Muslim members insisted that it be passed straightaway. Khwaja Nazimuddin, the Education Minister, was criticized for touring only predominantly Muslim districts of East Bengal and stirring communal feelings on the Bill. The debate took a communal turn, almost all Hindu members opposing the Bill and all Muslim members, with the exception of a few such as Fazlul Huq, supporting it. The Education Minister was accused of riding rough shod over the feelings of the Hindus and it was said that the passing of the Bill would be a glorious victory of the Muslims and Europeans over the Hindus. Kumar Sheb Shekhareswar Roy, Minister for local self-government, resigned on this issue.[63] There was a similar controversy over the United Provinces District Boards Primary Education Bill.[64]

Viewing educational questions in a communal spirit continued into the post-dyarchy era. Under the Government of India Act of 1935, elections to the provincial legislatures were held in 1937. In eight provinces, the Congress emerged as the largest party and formed the ministries, but it secured very few Muslim seats. Efforts to form Congress-League Coalition ministries in U.P. and Bombay were unsuccessful and Jinnah reorganised the Muslim League, reduced its fees and made a bid to popularise it among the masses. In March 1938, the Muslim League Council appointed a Committee to inquire into the "numerous complaints alleged to have reached its central office, concerning the hardships, ill-treatment and injustice that were meted out to Muslims in the Congress ruled provinces. Among the grievances listed was Gandhi's Basic Education scheme which was criticized as being anti-Muslim. Objection was raised to these schools being called *Vidya Mandirs*–temples of learning, and to Muslim children being obliged to honour the Congress flag, to join with folded hands in singing *Bande Mataram* and to wearing Gandhi caps.

In 1939, the All India Muslim Educational Conference appointed a committee with Nawab Kamal Jung Bahadur as Chairman to survey the educational system in India and to formulate a scheme for the education of Muslims with a view to "the preservation of the distinctive features of their culture and social order."[66] The Report of the Committee was published in 1942 and referred to the fears of a large number of educated Muslims that their separate cultural identity was being lost and submerged in a single Indian culture.

The notion that there was a danger of Muslims losing their

identity if they attended schools where education was secular and un-Islamic was not new. Hunter had expressed these sentiments in the 1870s.[67] The Indian Education Commission (1882) granted numerous special concessions to Muslims. The Calcutta University Commission (1917) had sought to safeguard the Muslim position all along the line.[68] The Hartog Committee (1929) appointed as an auxiliary committee of the Indian Statutory Commission, also urged that there should be special provisions for encouragement of Muslim education.

The British in India not only encouraged education of Muslims along separatist lines but also of non-Brahmins in Madras and Maharashtra and of other backward castes everywhere. The very idiom of British rule encouraged the development of political consciousness along communal lines and the education policy helped in this. For instance, the appointment of the Indian Education Commission in 1881 led to agitation over questions of eductation and the public services. Muslims wanted the Commission to recommend special scholarships and other concessions for them. Hindus wanted Urdu to be replaced by Hindi. Each community circulated petitions and held meetings to influence the government. Anjumans sponsored Muslims rallies while Hindu societies like the Arya Samaj were behind efforts to mobilize opinion in favor Hindi. The Census Reports made people increasingly aware of their caste and communal identity as also of their numerical strength or weakness. Among the various other devices of colonial rule which encouraged separatism, education policy was also of considerable importance in endowing different communities with a separate religious and social consciousness. Muslims, Hindus, Sikhs, were treated as distinct homogeneous entities. In the annual education reports of provincial government and of the Government of India, a special section was devoted to Muslim education.

Hindu and Muslim reformist and revivalist movements and denominational schools and colleges started by them encouraged education along separatist lines and the growth of communal consciousness.

Universities and schools were one important channel through which modernization penetrated Indian society. English education set off not one but a whole chain of reactions. Its political and social consequences were extremely subtle, complex and varied. The imbibing of western modes of thought led to greater participation in public activities and formation of political associations but these were often separatist in nature. Education, both traditional and modern, thus became a factor which contributed to the growth of communalism in India.

NOTES

1. A. Patwardhan and A. Mehta, *The Communal Triangle in India*, Allahabad, 1942. The Patwardhan–Mehta thesis is also argued by K.B. Krishna, *The Problem of Minorities in India*, London, 1939. Rajendra Prasad, *India Divided*. Beni Prasad, *The Hindu Muslim Question*, Allahabad, 1941.
2. A large number of British administrators-cum-scholars challenged the concept of Indian nationalism. It was a constant theme of Colonialist historiography that India was not a nation but a conglomeration of castes and communities. This view can be found in the Histories of India by James Mill, Mountstuart Elphinstone, Henry Elliot, Alfred Lyall, John Strachey and other. Among the Pakistani historians the best exponents of this view are I.H. Qureshi, *The Muslim Community of the Indo-Pakistan Subcontinent, 610-1947*. The Haque, 1962. Hafeez Malik, *Moslem Nationalism in India and Pakistan*, Washington D.C., 1963. Both K.M. Panikkar and Dr. R.C. Mazumdar reject the synthetic view of India's cultural development. See K.M. Panikkar, *A Survey of Indian History*, Bombay, 1956; R.C. Mazumdar, *Glimpses of Bengal in the Nineteenth Century*, Calcutta, 1960 and *History of the Freedom Movement in India*, 1, Calcutta, 1962.
3. K.K. Aziz, *The Making of Pakistan: A Study in Nationalism*. London, 1967, p. 18.
4. R.C. Majumdar, *Glimpses of Bengal in the Nineteenth Century*, Calcutta, 1960, p. 48.
5. W.C. Smith, *Modern Ismal in India*, London, 1946. A.R. Desai, *Social Background of Indian Nationalism*, Bombay, 1946.
6. D.N. Dhanagru, "Agrarian Conflict, Religion and Politics: The Moplah Rebellion in Malabar in the 19th and 20th Centuries", *Past and Present*, 1977, 74: 121-41. K.N. Panikkar and Stephen Dale have also written on the same theme. Sumit Sarkar, *The Swadeshi Movement in Bengal, 1903-1908*, P.P.H., New Delhi, 1973, p. 443 *et seq*.
7. Bipan Chandra, "The Role of Religion in the Rise and Growth of Communalism in Modern India".
8. P. Dixit, *Communalism, a Struggle for Power*, New Delhi, 1974. Francis Robinson, *Separatism among Indian Muslims*, Delhi, 1975. J.H. Broomfield. *Elite Conflict in a Plural Society, Twentieth Century Bengal*. Berkeley, 1968. Paul Brass, *Language, Religion and Politics in North India*, C.U.P., 1974. Mushirul Hasan, *Nationalism and Communal Politics in India*, Manohar, New Delhi, 1979. Anil Seal, *The Emergences of Indian Nationalism*, C.U.P., 1968.
9. Ayesha Jalal and Anil Seal, "Alternatives to Partition: Muslim Politics between the Wars", *Modern Asian Studies*, 15. 3. (1981). David Page, *Prelude to Partition: The Indian Muslims and the Imperial System of Control, 1920-32*.
10. N.B. Krishaa, *op. cit.* and Beni Prasad, *op. cit.*
11. Bipan Chandra, "The Hindu Tinge in Indian National Leadership and the Growth of Communalism in Modern India."
12. Bipan Chandraa, "Indian National Movement and the Communal Problem" in *Nationalism and Colonialism in Modern India*, New Delhi, 1979. Bimla Prasad,

"The Emergence of the Demand for India's Partition", *International Studies*, Vol. 8, No. 3, 1968, C.H. Philips, *India*, London, 1949.

13. Louis Dumont, "Nationalism and Communalism", *Contributions to Indian Sociology*, 1964, 7:30-70. Dr. Gyanendra Pandey in a recent articles has taken both leftist and liberal historians to task for neglecting religion in their studies of Communalism. G. Pandey, "Liberalism and the Study of Indian History". *E.P.W.*, 15 October 1983, Vol. XVIII, No. 42.
14. W.W. Hunter, *The Indian Musalmans*, 1871. For a recent exposition of this view see Rafiq Zakaria, *The Rise of Muslims in Indian Politics*, Bombay, 1970. Murray Titus, *Islam in India and Pakistan*, Calcutta, 1959.
15. Romila Thapar, Harbans Mukhia and Bipan Chandra, *Communalism and the Writing of Indian History*, New Delhi, 1969.
16. Hunter, *op. cit.*, p. 177.
17. J. Long, "The Social Condition of the Muhammedans and the Remedies". *Transactions of the Bengal Social Science Association*, i, ii (1868), p. 62.
18. *General Report of Public Instruction*, 1874-75, p. 100.
19. *General Report of Public Instruction*, 1875-76, p. 123.
20. In 1871, Muslims formed 13.5 per cent of the population of the North-Western Provinces and 9.9 per cent of the population of Oudh. The percentage of Muslim pupils in schools was 17.8 per cent and 25.3 per cent respectively. Selections from the Records of the Government of India, Home Department, *Correspondence on the Subject of the Education of the Muhammadan Community in British India and Their Employment in the Public Services Generally*, Calcutta, 1886, p. 355.
21. In 1881, of the total population, 85.97 per cent were Hindus and 13.74 Muslims but of the urban population, 64.5 per cent were Hindus and 34.6 per cent Muslims. *Report of the Census of the N.W.P. and Oudh, 1881*, pp. 59-60.
22. In 1921, of those engaged in agriculture, forestry and fishing 93.44 per cent were Hindus, only 6.01 per cent were Muslims. *Census of India, 1921, Vol. XVI. Pt. II*, 396-407. Only about 50 per cent Muslims followed agricultural pursuits, 25 per cent were in trade and 7 per cent in industry. *Census of India*, 1931, Vol. I, pt. 1, p. 30.
23. In 1886-87, 45.1 per cent or 235 out of 251 positions in the executive and judicial branches were held by Muslims. A. Seal, *Emergence of Indian Nationalism*, p. 118. As late as 1911 and 1921, Muslims held 41.94 per cent and 47.67 per cent of Government positions. *Census of India, 1921, Vol. XVI, pt. II*, pp. 396-407.
24. Number per 1,000 males

	Who are literate 1907	No. per 10,000 males literate in English 1907
Hindu Castes		
Namasudras	64	9
Rajbansis	60	6
Pods	183	29
Muslim Castes		
Dhobi	40	-
Julaha	52	-
Kulu	44	5

Census of India, 1911, Bengal, Vol. V. Pt. 1, p. 373.

25. In Bengal, for e.g. in 1931, while literacy per 1,000 males among Baidyas was 782, among Doms, a scheduled caste, it was 16. *Census of India, 1931, Vol. 1,*

pt.1, pp. 343-4.

26. In U.P., while 210 Sayyid males per 1,000 were literate and 227 per 10,000 literate in English, only 30 Juiahas per 1,000 were literate and 9 per 10,000 literate in English. *Census of India, 1921, U.P. Vol. XVI, Pt. I*, p. 126.
27. In the collegiate stage, Muslim pupils constituted 24.1 per cent of the total pupils, though Muslims formed 14.1 per cent of the population. *Progress of Educion in India, 1912-17, Vol. II*, p. 193.
28. John Strachey, *India: Its Administration and Progress*, p. 308.
29. *Progress of Education in India, 1907-12*, Vol. 1, p. 251.
30. Von Jurgen Lutt, *Hindu Nationalism in Uttar Pradesh, 1867-1900*, Stuttgart, 1970, p. 50.
31. Paul Brass, *op. cit.*, p. 131.
32. For instance, Choudhury Khaliquzzaman, *Pathway to Pakistan*, Lahore, 1961, Aziz Ahmad, *Islamic Modernism in India and Pakistan, 1857-1964*, O.U.O., 1967.
33. Jyotirindra Das Gupta, *Language Conflict and National Development*, Berkeley, 1970.
34. Paul Brass, *op. cit.*, p. 138.
35. *Indian Education Commission Report: Bengal Volume* (1884), pp. 213-17.
36. *Ibid*, p. 220.
37. *Aligarh Institute Gazette*, 5.4.1911.
38. M.S. Jain, *The Aligarh Movement*, Agra, 1965, Ch. 4.
39. See D. Lelyveld, *Aligarh's First Generation, Muslim Solidarity in British India*, Princeton, 1978. S.K. Bhatnagar, *History of M.A.O. College*.
40. Judicial and Public Despatches 2077/11, W. 1303/12, 1912, Vol. 1146.
41. For details of the Aligarh University see A. Basu, *Growth of Education and Political Development in India, 1898-1920*, O.U.P., 1974. pp. 161-174.
42. Education Proceedings, A (Confdl), August 1911, Proc. Nos. 1-2.
43. Education Proceedings, A (Confdl), March 1912, Proceeding Nos. 54-59.
44. Hardinge to Morley, 9-3-1911 and 29-3-1911. Hardinge Papers (117).
45. Enclosure to letter from Du Boulay to Sharp, 9-2-1912, Hardinge Papers, (83).
46. *Report of the Calcutta University Commission*, Vol. 1, pp. 153-4.
47. Zia-ul-Hasan Faruqui, *The Deoband School and the Demand for Pakistan*, Bombay, 1963. B. Metcalfe, *Islamic Revival in British India, Deoband, 1860-1900*, Princeton, 1982.
48. Firangi Mahal was the oldest of the leading schools in U.P. It was founded in the house of a French merchant (hence *Firaangi Mahal*) in Lucknow with a grant from Emperor Aurangzeb. The curriculum developed in this school, known as Dars-i-Mizamia, was adopted in most of the madrasas in India in one form or other. Nadwat-al-ulama was founded in 1894. Its prime mover was Abd-al-Ghafur, a Deputy Collector. Among its founders was Shibli Nomani, who was for some time at Aligarh and an associate of Sir Syed. Shibli Nomani was in control of Nadwat-al-ulama from 1904 to 1913.
49. V.A. Sundaram, ed., *Benares Hindu University*, 1905-1935, Benaras, 1936, pp. 3-4. See also S.L. Dar and S. Somaskandan, *History of Benares University*, Banares, 1966.
50. J.T.F. Jordens, *Swami Shraddhananda—His Life and Causes*, Delhi, O.U.P., 1981.
51. *Progress of Education in India, 1917-22, Vol. I*, p. 15. *Process of Education in India*, 1932-37, Vol. I, p. 5.
52. P. Hardy, *The Muslims of British India*. C.U.P., 1972, p. 205.
53. K. Mukerji, *Levels of Economic Activity and Public Expenditure in India*, London, 1965, pp. 83, 88, 93.

54. A detailed list of riots, numbers killed etc. is given in the *Report of the Indian Statutory Commission, Vol. IV, Pt. 1*, pp. 108-20.
55. *Progress of Education in Bengal, Seventh Quinquennial Review, 1922-1927*, p. 74.
56. *Ibid.*, p. 75.
57. *Progress of Education in India, 1922-27, Vol. I*, p. 242.
58. Rafiuddin Ahmad, *The Bengal Muslims, 1871-1900. A Quest for Identity*, O.U.P., Delhi, 1981.
59. *Bengal Education Reports, Seventh Quinquennial Review on the Progress of Education in Bengal, 1922-23 to 1926-27*, p. 74.
60. *Ibid.*, p. 75.
61. *Idem.*
62. *Ninth Quinquennial Review on the Progress of Education in Bengal for 1932-37*, p. 113.
63. *Bengal Legislative Council Proceedings, Vol. XXX, August 1930*, p. 238.
64. *Proceedings of the Legislattive Council of the United Provinces, February 1926*, pp. 434-87, 526-82, etc.
65. *Report of the Inquiry Committee appointed by the Council of the All India Muslim League to enquire into Muslim grievances in Congress Provinces, 1938.* (Commonly known as the Pirpur Report, as the Raja of Pirpur was Chairman of the Committee).
66. *Kamal Yar Jung Education Committee Report*, Calcutta, 1942.
67. *Indian Education Commission Report*, 1883-84.
68. *Calcutta University Commission Report*, op. cit.

6

INTERPRETING CANADIAN ECONOMIC DEVELOPMENT

H.V. Nelles

Canada is a rich, highly industrialized, but moderately troubled country. The qualifier seems all the more necessary at this distance. The 25 million people who presently inhabit its approximate 10 million square kilometers possess an economic power out of proportion to their small numbers. Canada, with less than half of one per cent of the world's population, produces four per cent of the world's total exports. Its Gross National Product of 253 billion US dollars in 1980 ranked it seventh amongst OECD countries behind the United States ($2,587), Japan ($1,040), Germany ($819), France ($651), Great Britain ($523) and Italy ($394).[1] Unstable exchange rates make more precise international comparisons more difficult, but in both Gross Domestic Product per capita and private consumption per capita Canada has usually stood among the world leaders. Wealth alone, of course, provides no immunity against the developmental anxiety.

The rate of Canadian growth has been, until recently, unusually brisk by world standards. Over the last century Canadian output has grown in real terms at an average rate of 40 per cent per decade, population by 19 per cent, and real domestic product per capita by 18 per cent. Tables 1 and 2 show the rough outlines of this growth decade by decade, while Table 3 offers comparisons with other rapidly growing economies. This sustained economic growth has transformed Canadian society and in the process endowed it with one of the highest standards of living in the world.

More than most developed countries, Canada depends upon trade to maintain these high levels of output and consumption. From the earliest European settlements in the 17th century until today, external trade has been a major factor in Canadian economic development. In recent years about 30 per cent of Canadian GNP has been generated by exports compared with about 20 per cent for OECD countries as whole. If anything, trade is becoming more important: exports as a percentage of Canadian GDP have risen over the past decade to current levels of approximately 25 per cent. Tables 4 and 5 provide a more detailed picture of the contemporary significance of trade in Canada compared with other industrialized economies. Not surprisingly, therefore, Canadian economic history has been above all a story of growth and trade.

The emergence of a group of small, relatively poor British colonies in the mid-19th century to membership in the select Group of Seven industrialized countries in that late 20th century is a success story by any standard. Like most such stories it has been told and retold many times in many different ways. From O.D. Skelton's optimistic narrative written at the height of Canada's first economic boom, through the classic interpretative accounts of W.A. Mackintosh and H.A. Innis in the 1930s to the more austere numerical estimation of Canada's national accounts by O.J. Firestone and Simon Kuznets in the 1950s, to the definitive compilation of the *Historical Statistics of Canada* (1965, revised and enlarged 1983), this growth and expansion has been measured, explained, and to a certain extent celebrated.[2]

Nevertheless, the quantitatively auspicious history of Canadian economic development is and always has been clouded by a fundamental doubt which is not usually encountered in similar advanced industrial countries. Concerning Canada's growth and relative wealth there is no question–opinion sharply divides–however, over the character and course of that development. The litmus test which differentiates the literature is the question: Is Canada an example of a normal industrial economy evolving towards maturity and a high degree of independence, or rather is it a case of distorted–albeit accelerated–dependent development? Industrial autonomy or richest colony; in which direction was Canada heading? That was a question which divided scholars who laid down the first analytic framework for the study of Canadian economic history in the 1920s and 1930s and it has continued to perplex their successors ever since. Moreover, it is a concern which transcends ideology: Marxist, orthodox, and most recently the new economic historians are internally split over this matter of fundamental orientation of development.

If the course of national economic development remains in doubt, so too the economic history of certain regions within the country raises unsettling anxieties. Canada is a large, sparsely populated country of diverse provincial societies. Though these interprovincial differences are not nearly as pronounced as those between states in India, they are nonetheless real and keenly felt.[3] Some provinces, especially those in the Atlantic region and the west–but for different reasons–have not fully shared in the broad national current of economic development. The Atlantic provinces have remained continuously poor and underdeveloped when measured against national averages. The Western provinces have prospered, but still perceive themselves marginalised by their small populations and on overdependence upon agriculture and natural resource extraction. Western wealth has been characterized by an extreme sensitivity to world commodity prices and a sense of powerlessness to affect national economic policies. Industrialization, its benefits and power, like the population, have been concentrated in the geographical centre of the country, Ontario, towards which the periphery constantly feels the tugs and resentments of dependence. Economic development in a Canadian context is thus a problem within a problem a question about the nature of growth, and a question about its internal distribution. Uneven growth nationally and regionally has spawned a host of Canadian discontents.

I

Where better to begin this introduction to the Canadian developmental neurosis than Graeme Wynn's wonderfully evocative book, *Timber Colony: A Historical Geography of Early Nineteenth Century New Brunswick*, recently published by the University of Toronto Press. This book takes us back to the very beginning of economic activity in Canada with the carving out of a community from the primeval forest. Of course there had been European settlement in the region for 200 years by the time Wynn's book begins; so, it is not the beginning in a chronological sense. But what Wynn observes of early New Brunswick could be said, mutatis mutandis, of those earlier colonies on the Atlantic coast and St. Lawrence river.[4]

"Forest, scarcely altered by the hand of man, spread over almost the entire province in 1800," Wynn reports. This magnificent forest, which was in many ways a barrier to economic development, nevertheless provided the settlers with their first commercial resource to exploit. Soon a regular trade in masts and ships' timbers sprang up, spurred by shortages resulting from the Napoleonic Wars. This trade continued on in peacetime, strengthened by a strong demand for domestic timber in Great Britain and a British tariff structure which discriminated in favour of colonial suppliers. Alongside this bulk timber trade a brisk commerce in sawn lumber developed to serve local needs, nearby New England demand, and ultimately British markets. Thus, within a few decades this former wilderness had been brought into an international flow of capital, population, information and trade.

Population increased steadily, though not spectacularly. Along the main river valleys lumbermen farmers and small parties of woodsmen financed by merchants in the port towns gradually pushed back the forest. Commercial agriculture took root in these clearings. Lumbering opportunities attracted merchants and capital, mainly from the United States, and immigrants, mainly from Ireland and Great Britain. By degrees, more efficient large scale capitalist timber operations displaced individual lumbermen, especially on the northern rivers. Immigration and high rates of natural increase provided the necessary reserve army of wage labourers upon which the industrial timber trade of the 1840s and 1850s depended. Wynn's book also describes in illuminating detail the equipment, techniques, labor force recruitment, organization, finance, and forwarding of this trade as well as its symbiotic relationship with agriculture.

In fifty years a complex society, riven with latent class, linguistic and religious antagonisms had taken form in New Brunswick on the strength of this international commerce in timber and sawn lumber. Let us take a step back from Wynn's account for a moment to get an overview of the situation. What had this commercial revolution wrought? In 1850 New Brunswick was still one of the smallest (population 193,000) British colonies. It remained entirely dependent upon external markets, vulnerable to price and demand changes in those markets, and dependent as well upon a rapidly depleting natural resource–the accessible prime timber had been quickly taken. Although more than 640,000 acres of land had been cleared by farmer-lumbermen, that was only a small fraction of the landscape. Wynn notes in his conclusion:

> In some areas well-cultivated fields stretched away from fertile intervals, but from many more vantage points almost unbroken forest ran back to the horizon. Little of New Brunswick had been obviously converted to man's purpose; even after Confederation, a natural historian could write of the province's vast forests that "embraced districts presenting all the features of primitive forests of other portions of the continent." And a traveller looking back on a tour through British North America might well have concluded that New Brunswick remained "comparatively a wilderness region."[5]

Nature, damaged but enduring, continued to dominate the landscape even after the commercial assault. At the end of Wynn's book New Brunswick remained as it was at the beginning and to a large extent remains to this day, heavily forested, thinly settled and comparatively poor. Development had swept through the region, plundering its resources, creating momentary wealth in the commercial nexus, but leaving a small, disadvantaged society to subsist in its wake. Commercial forestry did not seem to lay down the foundations of a permanent, dynamic, North American scale economy and society.

That image haunts the writing of Canadian economic history and, in recent years, the making of Canadian public policy. For without too much exaggeration, New Brunswick might be thought of by some scholars as a metaphor for Canada as a whole. It flourished on the extraction, crude processing, and export of natural resources to mature industrial economies. As the current White Paper on trade policy flatly observes: "In contrast to most industrialized countries, Canadian exports are heavily oriented towards resources or resource based products."[6] But what kind of society took shape under the aegis of such a trade in New Brunswick? What would become of such communities once demand shifted or the resources gave out? Here then is the developmental dilemma which has confronted Newfoundland fishermen, fur trading communities on the St. Lawrence, lumbermen and miners in the north and the mountains, Prairie grain farmers, and most recently oilmen in Alberta, all of whom have seen their resources dwindle and their external markets dry up.

But let us return to New Brunswick briefly, for its economic history did not end in 1850. Moreover, what followed provides a disturbing illustration of the inter-regional dimension of the development problem. The very last sentence of *Timber Colony* reads: "By 1850, the complex transition of society to modernity was underway in the still comparatively underdeveloped colony of New Brunswick." What of that transition? After Confederation in 1867, which created one large, federated colony out of four, the province of New Brunswick was gradually integrated into the newly created national market. The regional economy, which had previously looked outward to sea and trade, was re-oriented inwards towards the continent and the opportunities for growth presented by the economic union with Quebec, Ontario and later the West. How did the society respond to this challenge? For a time there was resistance and then some bitterness at the passing of a heroic age of "wooden ships and iron men." The economic history of the region was afterwards fashioned in the glow of this golden age nostalgia and the beginning of regional decline attributed to the new circumstances of Confederation. But thanks to the work of T.W. Acheson we know that the entrepreneurship, labour and capital of the region did begin to adjust successfully, especially following the adoption of a protective tariff in 1879. Nascent manufacturing industries were stimulated; new factories sprang up to serve the captive domestic market. Textile companies, food and beverage processors, a variety of consumers' goods as well as some producers' goods industries were located in the region. Coal and iron laid the groundwork for a major heavy industrial sector. What we now know of as the first product cycle phase of industrialization got under way. Indeed, during the 1880s the region was one of the most rapidly developing areas of the country.[7] Initially it seemed as if New Brunswick and its region would successfully manage the industrial transformation.

However, the transition proved transitory. Having no sooner embarked upon a course of industrialization, the bewildering process of de-industrialization began. Acheson shows that it was not the protective tariff but rather the nationalization of Canadian capitalism which worked against the region. Lacking a regional metropolitan centre with its own sphere of influence to protect, the Maritimes lost out to competition with other regions. In the late 19th century, manufacturing became more concentrated in Central Canada (Tables 6 and 7). Industrial production in the Maritimes failed to keep up with general trends; per capita income fell while local unemployment rose above national averages, and the region became a source of outmigrants bound for Upper Canada, the West and the United States (Table 8). Despite a high birth rate, for example, the population of New Brunswick remained almost constant from 1881 to the Second World War.[8] This tendency of industry and population to migrate to the centre was an entirely new and bewildering phenomenon. Acheson wrote of the period. Never before had the Maritimes confronted "a metropolis which devoured its children."[9]

The relative decline of the Maritime economy during the latter years of the 19th century and the beginning of the 20th illustrates both the problem of uneven development within Canada and intimates in a macrocosm the vulnerability of peripheral economies (such as Canada's) during the process of industrial restructuring. For some observers the problem within is serious enough, but the implications for the entire economy are even more ominous. Nor did federal government transportation or regional development policies (though none existed by that name at the time) respond in an attempt to even out interprovincial competition in such a geographically dispersed market. With occasional if grudging grants-in-aid to local governments and several commissions of inquiry to examine the causes of the economic malaise, the national government could safely ignore these regional discontents. Though there is some dispute over the efficacy of transportation subsidies as a remedy for the problem, it is nevertheless the case that not even this measure was deemed politically necessary.[10] "If one accepts that the basic objective of any country is to equalize opportunities across the land and to implement policies which ultimately turn regional disparities into positive advantages," concluded the late David Alexander, the most subtle and penetrating student of this question, "then the legitimate grievance of the Maritimes is that there was no place for it in twentieth century Canada."[11] And so the relative position of the Maritime economy deteriorated and the disparity which opened up was much wider than any experienced by the regions within the US economy.

Economic historians primarily concerned with growth and trade did not, understandably, devote much attention to the apparent anomaly of regional decline. But to the extent they did address the problem in passing, they tended to attribute the slow death of the Maritime economy to natural causes. S.A. Saunders, writing from the region in the 1930s, believed that nature and geography had forced the Maritimes "out of step" with the rest of the country. It was burdened with inadequate resources, a dispersed population geographically cut off from central and western markets, sub-scale industries, and marginal agriculture.[12] But on the face of it the region did not lack natural resources for it possessed waterpower, forests, coal and fisheries in abundance. W.A. Mackintosh, in his classic account of the growth and expansion of the national economy written at the end of the 1930s, thought it a problem not of a lack of resources, but the lack of the right kind of resources. While admitting that the protective tariff favoured Central Canadian industry at the expense of the Maritimes, Mackintosh believed the cause of economic decline to be much deeper. According to his analysis technological change and shifting international markets had "turned against the Maritimes in the last quarter of the nineteenth century." Having lost the traditional markets for fish, coal, ships and forest products, the region could not turn to the domestic Canadian market as a substitute.[13] In his view and that of later economists, not much could be done to alter these underlying circumstances, and thus the most logical course of alleviating the distress was to speed up scale-producing urbanization within the region and to encourage continued migration out of the region.[14] But let us not pursue the causes of what came to be known as Maritime economic backwardness any further, except to note that what has been said of the region also applies with equal force to the country.[15] Rather, let us return to the question of national development within which this regional problem is embedded.

II

The reason for falling resources and trade suspected in the case of Maritime decline is that in the classic interpretations of Canadian growth these were thought to be the major forces underlying growth and expansion. During the 1920s and 1930s, W.A. Mackintosh, an economist from Queen's University and later a senior civil servant, and H.A. Innis, a distinguished professor of Political Economy at the University of Toronto, separately and simultaneously worked out an explanatory framework for Canadian economic history. These two complementary interpretations both stressed the importance of staple products (narrowly defined as bulky, semi-processed, natural commodities with a high weight/volume ratio to value, produced for export) as the driving forces in Canadian development. They differed, however, over the implications of that analysis.

In an essay first published in 1923 in which Mackintosh attempted to assert the primacy of economic over political factors in the interpretation of Canadian development, he argued that: "The prime requisite of colonial prosperity is the colonial staple." He then briefly sketched in the history of the United States seen from that perspective and outlined the ups and downs of 19th century Canadian devepopment. He concluded with the most telling illustration of that proposition, the Canadian wheat boom of 1900 to 1913:

> A staple was exported to world markets; and, as southern cotton started the wheels of American industry and commerce in the nineteenth century, western wheat has permitted the initial step of the Canadian advance in the twentieth. It was only one commodity, and there were many; but it was the basis of that period of prosperity. The word staple primed the pump of Canadian industry.[16]

There in a nutshell was a theory of export-led growth in areas of recent settlement.

More than a decade later, in the depths of the Great Depression, Mackintosh expanded this outline into a full scale analytic narrative of Canadian economic history from 1867 to 1938 for a Royal Commission examining the fiscal and constitutional paralysis of the federation. Here in considerable detail Mackintosh cast Canadian development against a backdrop of changing technology and international demand which, at differential rates, valorized and permitted the exploitation of Canada's natural endowments. This demand for staple products carried with it a flow of capital and labour across the Atlantic. Within this shifting flow of material forces the Canadian government strove to create a transcontinental economy with its protective tariff, transportation, and immigration policies. As a combined result, Canada had industrialized quickly but at the cost of a heavy burden of debt and an incompletely fulfilled economic union. Mackintosh summarized the sources of Canadian growth as follows in his conclusion:

> Within the period of development which was of determining

> influence and up to the Great Depression, Canada experienced a rapid rate of expansion. The discovery of new resources, the tapping of new areas by transportation lines, a fructifying stream of capital imports, expanding export markets, and increased values given to resources by technological changes had promoted the expansion of population and industry. That expansion had proceeded in a framework of integrating national policies—policies designed to enlarge the internal circulation of goods and to increase the interdependence of the several regions.[17]

The export of resource staples had been the engine of Canadian growth.

Harold Innis elevated staples theory beyond economic analysis to an all embracing interpretation of Canadian economic, social and political development. Staple products not only drove the economy, in his view, they shaped the society and especially the state around them. In subtle but materially determined ways, societies took on the characteristics of the staples they produced. Innis' great contribution to Canadian history was to develop this insight in a series of major monographs, *A History of the Canadian Pacific Railway* (Toronto, 1923), *The Fur Trade in Canada* (Toronto, 1930), *The Cod Fisheries* (Toronto and New Haven, 1940), and more than a score of essays, introductions and scattered papers later collected in *Essays in Canadian Economic History* (Toronto, 1956). In rich, sometimes ponderous detail or in sparkling, evanescent suggestions, Innis explained how Canada developed on the strength of a succession of staple trades, from the cod fishery of the 16th and 17th centuries and the trade in beaver pelts which brought Spanish, English and French settlers to Canada in the first place, through the timber trade of New Brunswick and the Ottawa River during the early 19th century, the wheat staple of mid-19th century Ontario and early 20th century western Canada, to the non-ferrous metals, pulp and paper, and hydro-electric power sectors which Innis considered the new staples of the mid-20th centuries. Canada lurched forward from one staple-dominated era to another, and with each step institutions, social forms, fiscal pressures and external relations changed as well. In brief, Canada was but a series of *Timber Colonies*, with all the growth, exposure, and social dislocation that the term implied.

"The economic history of Canada," Innis wrote in 1930, "has been dominated by the discrepancy between the centre and the margin of western civilization. Energy has been directed toward the exploitation of staple products and the tendency has been cumulative."[18] Though the staple might change, certain broad features remained the same: external dependence upon markets, capital, migrants and technology, and the accumulation of overhead expenses–mainly for transportation improvements–which burdened succeeding stages with heavy fixed charges. Some staple products induced centralization and state intervention; others decentralization. But they all linked Canada firmly to more developed industrial nations. Here are just a few fragments by way of example to show how Innis used his analysis of economic phenomena to throw light on political events. Why did Canada remain within the British Empire long after it had been encouraged to go its own way? "Canada remained British in spite of free trade and chiefly because she continued as an exporter of staples to a progressively industrialized mother country." The appearance of new staple products in the first half of the 20th century entailed a reallocation of power within the federation: "The extension of the American empire, the decline of its natural resources, and the emergence of metropolitan areas, supported capitalist expansion in Canada and reinforced the trend of regionalism. The pull to the north and south has tended to become stronger in contrast with the pull east and west." The impact of the Great Depression, he explained at the time, was much more serious in Canada than most other countries because Canada had lost its essential foreign markets for wheat, pulp and paper and most minerals, but it retained the combined burden of interest on sunk capital and fiscal transfers associated with uneven growth: "Canada developed at the latest stages of modern industrialism and is among the first to feel the effects of the turn. The importance of the state, reliance on production of raw materials for export, particularly wheat, and the rigidities of continental development create serious problems of internal maladjustment as shown by quotas, bonuses, unemployment relief, the breakdown of federal provincial relations, and the like. . . . The basic position of overhead costs in the production of a small group of important staple commodities has involved the Canadian economy in a nose dive during the depression which has cut income in half."[19]

Innis and Mackintosh jointly framed the first and most enduring interpretation of Canadian economic development. Innis devoted most of his scholarly attention to the early staples, Mackintosh to the modern era. Innis ranged far beyond economic categories pressing the limits of the theory, while Mackintosh for the most part confined himself to economic trends and public policy. Their staples interpretation was eventually enshrined in the next generation by W.T. Easterbrook and H.G.J. Aitken's influential textbook, *Canadian Economic History*, published in 1958 and continuously in print ever since. As late as 1963 the theory was given a more rigorous theoretical formulation by M.H. Watkins.[20] The conception was so all embracing that regional economic historians, as we have seen in the case of the Maritimes, were compelled to work within it. Modified by Vernon Fowke and other western scholars, staples theory provided a basis for a critical assessment of national economic policies.[21] When two American academics zoomed into Canada in 1958 to assess the state of the economy–which they accomplished with the usual brusque efficiency–they observed that the literature relied rather heavily upon a few "great Canadian cliches," but they could not themselves unhorse the venerable staples.[22]

Although they agreed on the main outlines of the analysis, Innis and Mackintosh differed over evolutionary matters. Neither spent much time writing on the question, but remarks made in passing by the two authors admit of significantly different readings. Mackintosh was an optimist. He saw Canada moving through four stages of development as the phrase quoted earlier would suggest. First came initial settlement during which staple exports were absolutely essential. Then came stage two, the laying down of the transportation and institutional infrastructure on the basis of commodity production. During stage three the economy enters a phase of early industrialization behind tariff walls and the transition to maturity begins. The final stage, which Canada had yet to enter when he wrote, was full scale industrial maturity.[23] Innis was not as certain of this linear progression; at times he was downright pessimistic.

Canada's reliance upon commodity exports seemed, in his view, to be habit forming. Quite apart from the undue emphasis it gave one form of activity over others, the sheer weight of committed resources to staple production seemed to ensure a lengthening rather than a diminution of the lines of dependence. This is a phenomenon later writers came to refer to as 'the staples trap.'[24]

Innis himself did not write much about the question of industrial maturation except a few mordant paragraphs of regret at being drawn inexorably into the web of what he referred to in later years as "American imperialism." It seemed quite possible, in short, that staples production did not lead in linear fashion to industrial autarchy–as in the case of the United States–but rather continued subservience, albeit well paid, to imperial raw material requirements. In economic and political terms Canada may have freed itself from its former British orbit, only to become a satellite of a larger,, far more powerful and much more insidious neighbor. He described the transition being wrought by American capital after World War II by giving an old cliche an ironic twist: "Canada moved from colony to nation to colony."[25] Thus the founders of the "staples school" of Canadian historiography were ambivalent about the direction Canadian development seemed to be taking.

The quantitative revolution which swept the economics profession in the fifties and sixties did much to strip staples theory of it near mythic power. In 1958 Kenneth Buckley expressed frustration with the imprecision of the theory and openly questioned its ability to explain growth after the passing of the fur trade. In his own monograph, published in 1955, he argued on the basis of elaborately detailed indices that domestic capital formation was the driving force of the economy in the late 19th and early 20th centuries.[26] G.W. Bertram, in the early 1960s, further added to the scepticism. The statistical time series he compiled on the growth of Canadian manufacturing failed to show any sharp discontinuities consistent with the hypothesis that wheat had given the economy a massive jolt.[27] Then in 1966 E.J. Chambers and D.F. Gordon uttered the ultimate heresy, arguing on the basis of a clearly specified theory that the wheat boom probably accounted for only a relatively insignificant (8 per cent) proportion of the growth of the Canadian economy between 1901 and 1911.[28] This iconoclastic finding was, of course, immediately and furiously challenged. In the course of a long debate– which is still going on–the Chambers and Gordon theory has been modified and new data introduced. Currently it is probably fair to say that revisionists put the contribution of the wheat staple closer to 20 per cent, a significant figure to be sure, but clearly other factors were more important.[29] Similarly, other corners of the staples edifice have crumbled under rigorous theoretical and empirical testing.[30]

The progressive demolition of staples theory without a comparable effort at construction of a new synthesis has left the field in a state of confusion. Thus it was possible for two new textbooks in Canadian economic history appearing in 1980 and 1981 to arrive at quite different conclusions about the character of Canadian development. W.L. Marr and D.G. Paterson adopted a modified staples approach, duly tricked out with modern theoretical and quantitative embroidery, in their influential textbook, *Canada: An Economic History* (Toronto, 1980). They eschew grand schemetizing a la Innis, but they do find the export-led model of growth useful in an industrializing country with such large agricultural and natural resource sectors. Indeed they discover the missing staple (dairying and stock raising) upon which to establish late 19th century expansion. In justice, the main objective of their book is to provide historical illustration for contemporary theoretical maxims. They build up a picture of the economy with topical layers (population, labour force, capital formation, transportation, commercial policy and so forth) without laying great stress upon a single underlying story. Nevertheless, the emphasis they put upon export-led growth and the unusual allocation of an entire chapter to the distorting effects of high levels of foreign investment in certain sectors aligns them comfortably within the Innis tradition of ambivalence about the course of Canadian development.

Richard Pomfret, in a textbook published a year later, dispensed completely with staples theory as well as Marxist, Rostowian and economic backwardness approaches to the subject. Surveying this interpretative wreckage Pomfret notes laconically: "This leaves modern (post 1850) Canadian economic history without a generally accepted analytical framework." That was just as well, for he did not think there was anything unique about Canada which required a special theory. For him, Canada presented a case of perfectly straightforward industrialization along European or American lines. "In sum, after taking account of the resource endowment, geography and the timing of the industrial revolution," he concluded, "Canada's post-industrial economic expansion has been similar to that of other countries."[31] Pomfret, then, may be thought of as the legitimate heir of Mackintosh.

Canadian economic history has undergone a thorough methodological revolution in the last decade. Pomfret, Marr and Paterson are all "new" economic historians who require explicit theory, quantitative evidence, and mathematical proofs. They generally agree on many of the debates internal to the field. But they differ on the fundamental question of the direction of Canadian development.

The Left in Canada has not been well represented in the literature of economic development until recently. However, an examination of earlier political analysis and more recent scholarly writing reveals a similar rift.

Canada has always presented something of a problem to Marxists. The difficulty has been especially acute for orthodox Marxists. What was Canada, a political and economic colony, or a fully developed capitalist state? Did a national bourgeoisie come to power, or did Canada remain under the dominance of metropolitan capital? For the Communist Party of Canada, of course this has been a crucial strategic question. In the 1920s the party declared Canada a colony of Great Britain, from which it followed that it should support the bourgeois struggle for independence. Canada's political and economic history were then fitted into that analysis. On the platform, national liberation became "a step towards a Workers' and Farmers' Republic.[32] In 1928 and 1929, however, the Communist-International instructed the Canadian party to change its line:

> On the basis of Canada's development into a definite capitalist country the Party must put emphasis on the Canadian bourgeoisie as the main enemy of the Canadian proletariat. The ties between Canada and the British Empire are not ties of compulsion but of mutual interests in exploitation . . . the Canadian proletariat therefore cannot attribute to the Canadian bourgeoisie the role of an anti-imperialist class fighting for national freedom and a bourgois-democratic republic.[33]

Thus, for the purposes of the Communist Party, the revolution had occurred and independence attained sometime between 1926 and 1928. The Party dutifully turned to confront Canadian capital and history was rewritten to emphasize the domestic class struggle. It is within this broad context that Stanley Ryerson conceived his two part history of Canada up to the 1870s. Accordingly, he was one of the few Canadian historians to place great emphasis upon the emergence in the St. Lawrence valley in the mid-nineteenth century of significant industrial activity. For him the political union of Confederation represented the partial assumption of state power by this industrial class.[34]

In the late 1940s the Communist Party revived the nationalist, anti-imperialist line, this time against US economic and military penetration. It did so in response to the global response of Communism to the Cold War, but the essential analysis of Canadian development did not change. A nascent bourgeoisie had taken control over the economy and the state, but unaccountably this class had begun to sell out the former to US industrialists. One historian of the movement cites the gradual appearance of articles in the party newspapers re-interpreting Canadian history to stress its anti-American aspects after 1948, but he adds, "much of this had a curiously non-class character."[35]

Canadian social democrats have not felt the compulsion to locate themselves within the broad sweep of history or justify their actions in historical terms. When social democrats wrote history, it was mainly about themselves, to perhaps ensure for themselves a place in history. Their concerns were mainly with their intellectual precursors, origins, saintly leaders, internal factions, electoral struggles, legislative achievements, relations with the trade union movement, and battles with the Communists.[36] The CCF Party, which coalesced in the mid-thirties, assumed that a distinctive Canadian capitalism existed, pledged itself in its most feisty moments towards its eradication and replacement by what was called a cooperative commonwealth. In practice that meant the creation of a regulatory, welfare state characterized by a large public sector. This socialist party (renamed the New Democratic Party in 1961 following an organic alliance with the trade unions) was concerned, but not obsessed by, foreign economic and political influence. The CCF and the NDP believed that the struggle for social justice was essentially a struggle between Canadians and that democratic socialism was possible in one country as it had been in one province.

The late sixties witnessed the rise of several varieties of nationalism in the arts, the media, the universities, the unions, and the three major political parties. It began with a campaign against nuclear weapons, developed into a critique of US foreign policy, racism and imperialism during the war in Viet Nam, and then became internalized with a reaction against Canadian complicity in that war, the progressive "Americanization" of Canadian culture and institutions, and especially growing US control over the Canadian economy. On the left wing of the ruling Liberal Party, Walter Gordon led a movement to halt what was referred to as "continentalism" and promote increased Canadian ownership. On the right, George Grant's influential lament for the demise of what he imagined to be a conservative culture under a pall of US technology and liberalism, inspired an amorphous group of Progressive Conservative nationalists to think of themselves as Red Tories.[37] The analysis of these and other nationalisms of the period I leave to others. One variant, however, is of considerable interest. A group of scholar-activists, loosely referred to as "left-nationalists," advocated economic nationalism with particular vigor and, more relevant to the discussion here, completely re-interpreted Canadian economic history in the process.

The first substantial statement from this quarter took the form of Kari Levitt's phenomenally successful tract, *Silent Surrender* (Toronto, 1970), which documented for a wide audience the full extent of foreign and especially US ownership.[38] What was novel about her book, however, was the historical setting in which she interpreted the well-known statistics. A developmental economist with experience in the Caribbean and the daughter of Karl Polanyi, the eminent economic historian, she argued that Canada had been steadily re-colonized from the 1920s onward, but especially after World War II, by the "new mercantilism of direct investment." Like many other countries, Canada had been drawn inexorably into a new form of dependence within a new kind of informal empire. US multinational corporations had occupied the commanding heights of high technology manufacturing and dominated the resource sector. This on the one hand had endowed Canada with an inefficient, miniature replica of US industrial sector, unable to compete internationally, and on the other distorted the economy in the interests of supplying resources and raw materials to the United States. As a by-product, the process of regionalization and political fragmentation had been encouraged by foreign penetration. In all, Canada's excessive dependence upon foreign capital and reliance upon primary products exports, Kari Levitt argued, gave Canada the external profile of the richest, underdeveloped country in the world.

These themes of underdevelopment, neo-mercantilism, and destiny denied were then reworked by others into a powerful historical explanation of dependence and a political programme for an independent socialist Canada. Ironically, just as mainstream economists discarded staples theory, these neo-Marxist nationalists rediscovered this uniquely Canadian contribution to the international literature of development and made it the foundation of their new history of Canada's permanent dependence. This grafting of Marxist analysis onto the old trunk of orthodox historiography made sense despite the ironies, argued M.H. Watkins, one of the founders of the new school:

> While its (staple theory's) leading proponents were certainly liberals, at least in the beginning it was clearly political economy and at least in the hands of Innis it was about dependence–and these latter two characteristics are, of course, central to Marxists. Innis in particular was a liberal with a difference, who saw the dark underside and gross contradictions and this makes him susceptible to an approach that specializes in such matters.[39]
>
> At no stage have native Canadian inudstrialists who profited from the production and sale of manufactured good dominated Canadian capitalism. This central fact has flowed from the weakness of Canadian capitalism in relation to that of outside imperialist countries. Dependency has shaped the character of Canadian capitalism and has created a capitalist class that has needed continued dependency for its continued well-being.

To the bill of particulars against American investment in Canadian manufacturing and resource development–a long list which included a loss of sovereignty, permanent balance of payments problems, a truncated industrial structure, sub-scale branch plants without world product mandates, political fragmentation, low levels of manufactured exports, and a continental labour movement–Watkins and Laxer added the spectre of de-indsutrialization: "The cost of the loss of control of the Canadian state to American corporations is now increasingly clear to Canadians; in a period of inter-imperialist rivalry and a crisis of overproduction for the United States, it means de-industrialization for Canada." It followed, therefore, that if "American capitalism is the ultimate power in the Canadian state," the first step in the class struggle was to seek national liberation.[41] Since the business class was so emasculated, Watkins argued, "nationalism for Canada must mean, and can only mean, a nationalism of the left."[42]

In a remarkable burst of collective energy, the history and sociology of Canada were suddenly re-interpreted from this perspective.

Wallace Clement outlined the nature of first the Canadian and then the overriding Continental bourgeoisie. Martin Robin used staples theory to explain the polarized class politics of a resource dependent province, British Columbia. The Milners rewrote the history of French Canadians in Quebec, a people doubly colonized by the US and English Canada. Henry Weltmeyer and R.J. Sacouman applied these new notions of permanent dependence to the internal problem of Maritime underdevelopment.[43] It should be noted that some of this was history (and sociology) written on the run for use in an on-going political struggle rather than history for its own sake. Secondly, the critique was initially shaped without reference to the international literature of dependency theory associated with Andre Gunder Frank. Only afterwards was this supportive scholarship incorporated and Canada given a history more directly aligned with African and south American development.[44]

This left-nationalist conception of dependent, distorted development came under a withering cross-fire of criticism from academic historians,[45] but more particularly from writers associated with the orthodox left. Stanley Ryerson condemned the almost wilful misreading of Marx, the exaggeration of merchant capitalism, the neglect of nascent industrialism, and the indifference to the local class struggle which characterized an approach he considered "a warped mercantilist dogmatism tacitly at war with Marxism." L.R. Macdonald delivered a devastating blow to Naylor's distinction between merchant capital on the one hand and industrial capital on the other in late 19th century Canada. Others attempted to differentiate Canadian development from the patterns associated with the Third World. In sum, the old left reaffirmed that Canada was indeed an advanced, capitalist society, "no matter what percentage of Canadian industry is US owned. The nationalist question is for the most part a non-issue," as Simon Rosenblum insisted.[46]

Jorge Niosi, a sociologist from the University of Quebec at Montreal, has done the most constructive work on the left to establish the argument that Canada (and Quebec) does indeed possess a national, dominant, bourgeoisie. In his first book, translated as *The Economy of Canada: Who Controls It?* (Montreal 1978), he refuted the notion of control of the economy by finance capitalists, arguing instead that Canada had a broadly based "ruling class" which shared power with US interests. In his second book, *La Bourgeoisie Canadienne: La Formation et le developpment d'une classe dominante* (Montreal, 1980), Niosi concluded as his title would suggest that the Canadian bourgeoisie was not essentially comprador. While not wishing to deny completely the importance of dependence and underdevelopment, Niosi sought to place the emphasis of critical analysis where he thought it should be, on the development of social classes within Canada: *J'ai voulu montrer qu'il existe au Canada une bourgeoisie autochtone tres robuste, bien que travaillee par des clivages regionaux et ethniques, et par des luttes entre le grand et le petit capitalism local.*[47] Similarly Glen Williams, a political scientist from Carleton University, has dismissed the analytical framework of Third World dependency theory. In his new book, *Not For Export: Towards a Political Economy of Canada's Arrested Industrialization* (Toronto, 1983), Williams locates an explanation for the penetration of foreign capital in the manufacturing sector on the one hand, and the extremely poor record of manufactured exports on the other (Table 9), in the inherent contradictions of a strategy of import substitution industrialization adopted by the Canadian bourgeoisie and enshrined by the state in Canada's tariff structure for the last century.

Much more could be said about these and other views of Canadian development on the left. We seem to be entering what might be called the postnationalist phase of analysis in the study of Canada's economic history. New lines of communication are being drawn between socialist and, for example, traditional neo-classical interpretations as the tariff rather than staples assumes responsibility for the distortions of Canadian development.[48] But it is enough for our purposes here to observe the fundamental cleavage which on the left, as elsewhere, divides those who conceived of Canada as a normally evolving economy and those who thought the apparent distortions difficult to account for within the orthodox frame of Marxian analysis.

IV

In this brief overview we have seen that the unbalanced character of Canadian economic development has raised some doubt, especially in the historiography of peripheral regions, about the linearity of the developmental process. These anxieties have also been seen to trouble the classical exponents of the staples theory of Canadian development, their revisionist successors, as well as interpreters on the left.

This basic dichotomy could be expanded to embrace contemporary debates about national macro-economic policy, the necessity of an "industrial strategy," the question of Quebec, and the future course of western Canadian economic development. In this last instance, for example, it could be shown that the fear of life after the resources have been used up has inspired vigorous "province building" through public and private agencies.[49]

However, any such classification scheme necessarily slights work which has for one reason or another remained indifferent to the question. It does not do justice, for example to the extremely important work that has been done in colonial economic history, quantitative analysis and labour history.[50]

Nevertheless, the interpretative division outlined in this paper serves to underline the hybrid nature of Canadian development. Canada falls clearly within the broad pattern of western industrialization–seen from either a Marxist or non-Marxist perspective–but it has a sufficiently strong tinge of dependency to provide links with the economic history of regions on the margins of industrialization at the core. For this reason the most fruitful approach to Canadian economic history in the future will be to transcend the reigning Euro-American focus of implicitly archetypical development by comparing Canada explicitly with processes at work in smaller European economies, Brazil, Mexico, Argentina, Japan and, perhaps, India.[51]

NOTES

1. OECD, Economic Survey, *Canada* (Paris, 1983), pp. 59 ff.
2. O.D. Skelton, *General Economic History of the Diminion* (Toronto, 1913); W.A. Mackintosh, *The Economic Background of Dominion Provincial Relations* (Ottawa, 1939, reprinted Toronto, 1964); O.J. Firestone, *Canada's Economic Development* (London, 1958); Simon Kuznets, *Modern Economic Growth* (New Haven, 1966); for another perspective on Canada's comparative growth see Angus Madison, *Economic Growth in the West* (New York, 1964).
3. For views of regional differences from a politicl, geographical and economic perspective repectively, see D.J. Elkins and R. Simeon, *Small Worlds* (Toronto, 1980); L.D. McCann, ed., *Heartland and Hinterland* (Toronto, 1983); and Paul Phillips, *Regional Disparities* (Toronto, 1978).
4. A.H. Clark, *Acadia* (Madison, 1968); Grant Head, *Eighteenth Century Newfoundland* (Toronto, 1976); E. Salone, *Lacolonisation de la Nouvelle France* (Paris, 1905); M. Trudel, *The Beginnings of New France* (Toronto, 1980); R.C. Harris, *The Seigneurial System in Early Canada* (Madison, 1968).
5. Wynn, *Timber Golony*, p. 150.
6. Canada, Department of External Affairs, *A Review of Canadian Trade Policy*

(Ottawa, 1983), p. 25.

7. T.W. Acheson, "The national Policy and the Industrialization of the Maritimes, 1880-1910," Acadiensis, Vol. I, 1972, pp. 3-28.
8. M. Urquhart, K. Buckley and F.H. Leacy, eds., *Historical Statistics of Canada* (Second Edition, Ottawa, 1983), Series A-2.
9. Acheson, rom *op. cit.*, p. 28.
10. E.R. Forbes, *The Maritime Rights Movement* (Montreal, 1979); and essays by Forbes and Acheson in D.J. Bercuson, ed., *Canada and the Burden of Unity* (Toronto, 1977).
11. David G. Alexander, *Atlantic Canada and Confederation* (Toronto, 1983), p. 73. This is a posthumous collection of his essays written mainly during the 197s.
12. S.A. Saunders, *Studies in the Economy of the Maritime Provinces* (Toronto, 1939) and *The Economic History of the Maritime Provinces* (Ottawa, 1939).
13. W.A. Mackintosh, *The Economic Background to Dominion-Provincial Reletings* (Ottawa, 1939, reprinted Toronto, 1964), pp. 82-7, 153-4.
14. P. Copes, (St. John's, 1961), and *The Resettlement of Fishing Communities in Newfoundland* (Ottawa, 1972).
15. Contemporary economists discount both resource endowments (see L. Copithorne, "Natural Resources and Regional Disparities: A Sceptical View," *Canadian Public Policy* Vol. V, 1979, pp. 181-94) and industrial structure arguments (see L. Auer, *Regional Disparities of Productivited Growth in Canada* (Ottawa, 1979)). Instead they attribute most of the income disparity to low levels of productivity associated with lower skilled, less technologically equipped labour (see for example, Economic Council of Canada, *Living Together* (Ottawa, 1977), and Auer, *op. cit.* In short they have shifted the blame from the land to the people of the region. This is not a view widely shared in the region. For a comparable discussion of the productivity deficiencies of Canada in an international perspective see the Economic Council of Canada "productivity report," sadly mistiled, *The Bottom Line* (Ottawa, 1983).
16. Mackintosh, "Economic Factors in Canadian History," reprinted in W.T. Easterbrook and M.H. Watkins, eds., *Approaches to Canadian Economic History* (Toromo, 1967), pp. 4, 14.
17. Mackintosh, *The Economic Background to Dominion-Provincial Relations*, p. 179.
18. H.A. Innis, *The Fur Trade in Canada* (Toronto, 1956 edition), p. 386
19. Ibid., p. 386; M.Q. Innis, ed., *Essays in Canadian Economic History* (Toronto, 1956), pp. 134 , 209. The best commentary on Innis' historical writing is found in C. Berger, *The Writing of Canadian History* (Toronto, 1978). Comparative data concerning the relative impact of the Great Depression and the recent severe recession can be found in Tables 10 and 11.
20. M.H. Watkins, "A Staple Theory of Economic Growth," reprinted in Easterbrook and Watkins, op. cit., pp. 49-73.
21. V.C. Fowke, *The National Policy and the Wheat Economy* (Toronto, 1957), and "The National Policy — Old and New," reprinted in Easterbrook and Watkins, op. cit., pp. 237-58.
22. R.E. Caves and R.H. Holton, *The Canadian Economy: Prospect and Retrospect* (Combridge, 1959), p. xiii.
23. This line of analysis was suggested by M. Watkins in "The Staple Theory Revisited," *Journal of Canadian Studies*, Vol. XII, 1977, pp. 83-95, and is developed in Glen Williams, *Not For Export: Towards a Political Economy of Canada's Arrested Industrialization* (Toronto, 1983), pp. 130-7.

24. See pp. 111-114 of this book.
25. *Essays in Canadian Economic History*, p. 405.
26. "The Role of Staple Industries in Canada's Development," *Journal of Econmic History*, Vol. 18, 1958, pp. 439-50; *Capital Formation in Canada, 1896-1930* (Toronto, 1955).
27. "Economic Growth and Canadian Industry, 1870-1915: The Staple Model and the Take-off Hypothesis," *Canadian Journal of Economics and Political Science*, Vol. XXIX, 1963; pp. 162-84; and "Historical Statistics on Growth and Structure of Manufacturing in Canada, 1870-1957," in J. Henripin and A. Asimakopolous, eds., *Canadian Political Science Association Conference on Statistics 1962 and 1963* (Toronto, 1964), pp. 93-146.
28. "Primary Products and Economic Growth: An Empirical Measurement," *Journal of Political Economy*, Vol. 75, 1966, pp. 315-32.
29. References to specific countributions to this debate can be found in the bibliographies in R. Pomfret and Marr and Paterson listed below and in T. Dick, *Economic History of Canada: A Guide to Information Sources* (Detroit, 1979).
30. For example, Ann Carlos, "The Birth and Death of a Predator: Competition in the North American Fur Trade," *Explorations in Economic History*, Vol. 19, 1982, pp. 156-83, and W.J. Eccles, "A Belated Review of Harold Adams Innis, *The Fur Trade in Canada*," *Canadian Historical Review*, Vol. LX, 1979, pp. 419-41.
31. R. Pomfret, *The Economic Development of Canada* (Toronto 1981), p. 202.
32. G. Van Houten, et al., *Canada's Party of Socialism: A History of the Communist Party of Canada, 1921-1976* (Toronto, 1982), pp. 60-4, 175-91, and N. Penner, *The Canadian Left: A Critical Analysis* (Toronto, 1977), pp. 86-108. I am indebted to my friend Professor Joseph Levitt for help with this section.
33. Quoted in Penner, op. cit., p. 92.
34. S. Ryerson, *Unequal Union* (Toronto, 1968).
35. Penner, op. cit., p. 105.
36. There is a vast literature on the CCF-NDP. See inter alia, W. Young, *Anatomy of a Party* (Toronto, 1971), K. McNaught, *A Prophet in Politics* (Toronto, 1963), G. Horowitz, *Canadian Labour in Politics* (Toronto 1968), D. Morton,*NDP: The Dream of Power* (Toronto, 1974) and Ivan Avakumovic Socialism in Canada (Toronto, 1978).
37. Denis Smith, *Gentle Patriot* (Edmonton, 1973); Walter Gordon, A. Political Memoir (Toronto, 1977); G. Grant, *Lament for a Nation* (Toronto, 1965) and *Technology and Empire* (Toronto, 1969). The best critical review of Grant is R. Cook, *The Maple Leaf Forever* (Toronto, 1971), pp. 46-67. The currents of economic and cultural nationalism can be sampled in A. Rotstein and G. Lax, *Independence: The Canadian Challenge* (Toronto, 1972), I. Lumsden, ed., *Close the 49th Paralles* (Toronto, 1970) and disdained in R. Bothwell, I. Drummond, and J. English, *Canada Since 1945* (Toronto, 1981).
38. Curiously politically initiated investigation pre-dated and provided the groundwork for later academic analysis. The key documents are M. Watkins et al., *Foreign Ownership and the Structure of Canadian Industry* (Ottawa, 1968), The *Eleventh Report of the Standing Committee on External Affairs and national Defence Respecting Canada-US Relations* (Ottawa, 1970) and *Foreign Direct Investment in Canada* (Ottawa, 1972).
39 M. Watkins, 'The Staple Theory Revisited,' p. 83.
40. *The History of Canadian Business* (Toronto, 1975), Vol. II, pp. 283-4.
41. "Introduction to the Political Economy of Canada," in R. Laxer, ed, *(Canada) Ltd. The Political Economy of Dependency* (Toronto, 1973), pp. 29, 35, 37. For ownership data see Table 12.

42. Quoted in J. Layton, "Nationalism and the Canadian Bourgoisie: Contradictions of Dependence," *Canadian Review of Studies in nationalism 1976*, p. 146. see also Watkins' essay in R. Laxer, op. cit., pp. 107-26.
43. Wallace Clement, *The Canadian Corporate Elite* (Toronto, 1975) and *Continental Corporate Power* (Toronto, 1978); Martin Robin, *The Company Province* (Toronto, 1972-3),2 vols; H. and S. Milner, *The Decolonization of Quebec* (Toronto, 1973) and R.J. Brym and R.J. Sacouman, eds., *Underdevelopment and Social Movements in Atlantic Canada* (Toronto, 1979).
44. . Naylor, "Comentary," *Our Generation*, Vol. 11, 1975, pp. 17-25.
45. Among the more tthoughtful D. McCalla's might be counted, 'Tom Naylor's *A History of Canadian Business, 1867-1914: A Comment*,' Canadian Historical Association, *Historical Papers*, 1976, pp. 249-54.
46. Simon Rosenblum, "Economic Nationalism and the English Canadian Socialist Movement," ibid., pp. 5-17; S. Ryerson, "Who's Looking After Business," *This Magazine*, November-December 1976, pp. 41-7, and L.R. MacDonald, "Merchants Against Industry: An Idea and Its Origins,"*Canadian Historical Review*, Vol. LVI, 1976, pp. 263-81.
47. Niosi, *La Bourgoisie*, pp. 10-11.
48. For the longest time the tariff was the chief villian in Canadian economic history, at least as seen by economists; see J. Dales, *The protective Tariff in Canada's Economic Development* (Toronto, 1966). For business justification see J.M. Bliss, *A Living Profit* (Toronto, 1974).
49. An excellent discussion of this can be found in J.Richards and L. Pratt, *Prairie Capitalism: Power and Influence in the New West* (Toronto, 1979).
50. Examples of the first would include, Fernand ouellet, *Histoire Economique et Social du Quebec* (Montreal, 1966). D. McCalla, *The Upper Canada Trade* (Toronto, 1980) and A.J. Ray, *indians and the Fur Trade* (Toronto, 1974); of the second, K. Norrie, "The Rate of Settlement of the Canadian Prairies, 1870-1911," *Journal of Economic History*, Vol. 35, 1975, pp. 410-27, and Alan Green, *Regional Aspects of Canada's Economic Growth* (Toronto, 1971) and *Immigration and the Post-War Canadian Economy* (Toronto, and the last, Greg Kealey, *Toronto Workers Respond to Industrial Capitalism, 1867-1892* (Toronto, 1980), Bryan Palmer, *A Culture in Conflict: Skilled Workers and Industrial Capitalism in Hamilton, Ontario, 1860-1914* (Montreal, 1979), and G. Kealey and B. Palmer, *Dreaming of What Might Be: The Knights of Labor in Ontario, 1880-1900* (New York, 1982).
51. In this enterprise work such as Peter Evans' *Dependent Development* 9princeton, 1979) and A.D. Chandler and H. Daems, eds., *Managerial Hierarchies* (Cambridge, 1980) to take two quite different examples should prove useful.

TABLE 1

Long-Terms Trends in GNP, Real GNP, and Real GNP Per Capita, 1850-1970 (1935-39 prices = 100)

Year (1)	GNP (2) (5 millions)	Real GNP (3) (5 millions)	Real GNP Per Capita (4) (5 millions)
1850	169	406	167
1860	319	582	180
1870	459	764	211
1880	581	981	231
1890	1,803	1,366	286
1900	1,057	1,877	354
1910	2,138	3,085	441
1920	5,5,43	3,844	449
1930	5,728	5,119	501
1940	6,743	6,743	592
1950	18,006	10,475	764
1960	36,287	19,199	1,074
1970	85,685	33,732	1,578

TABLE 2

Growth of Income, 1851-1970: Compound Average Annual Rates of Growth Per Decade (1935-39 prices = 100)

Period	GNP	Price Level	Real GNP	Real GNP Per Capita
(1)	(2)	(3)	(4)	(5)
1851-60	7.81	0.10	4.08	0.87
1861-70	8.71	0.92	2.76	1.58
1871-80	2.38	-0.17	2.53	0.90
1881-90	3.29	-0.07	3.37	2.17
1891-1900	2.97	-0.43	3.23	2.15
1901-10	7.78	2.10	5.56	2.68
1911-20	9.48	7.60	1.74	-0.36
1921-30	0.34	-2.50	2.92	1.12
1931-40	1.61	-1.12	2.76	1.65
1941-50	10.66	5.57	4.83	2.89
1951-60	7.57	0.95	6.55	3.77
1961-70	8.34	2.96	5.19	3.36

Source: W.L. Marr and D.G. Paterson, *Canada: An Economic History* (Toronto, 1980), pp. 6, 19.

TABLE 3

Rates of Growth in total Product, Population, Product per Capita and Product per Man-hour, Developed Countries, Two long Periods, 1870-1913 (I) and 1913-60 (II) percentages per decade)

	Total products I	Total products II	Population I	Population II	Product per capita I	Product per capita II	Product per man-hour I	Product per man-hour II
	(1)	(2)	(3)	(4)	(5)	(6)	(7)	(8)
1. United Kingdom	24.4	20.7	9.2	4.5	13.9	15.5	16.3	19.5 (20.2)
2. France	16.9	15.7	1.8	1.9	14.9	16.6	19.6	23.0 (20.2)
3. Germany, FR (1871)	33.2	28.4	12.4	9.4	18.5	17.4	22.7	21.6 (20.4)
4. Belgium	30.5	15.1	10.0	3.8	18.7	10.8	22.3	18.0 (14.4)
5. Switzerland (1890)	26.7	29.8	11.8	7.2	13.4	21.1	16.7	20.7 (25.0)
6. Netherlands (1900)	24.8	30.1	15.0	14.2	8.5	13.9	11.4	18.2 (17.1)
7. Denmark	37.0	26.1	11.2	9.4	23.2	15.2	28.7	19.4 (18.7)
8. Norway	23.7	32.3	8.3	8.5	14.2	21.9	19.3	30.7
9. Sweden	33.9	27.5	7.2	6.3	24.9	20.0	30.2	25.4 (24.5)
10. Italy (1890)	15.0	25.4	6.8	6.8	7.7	17.4	12.9	26.1 (22.1)
10a. Italy (1890)	22.6	25.4	6.9	6.8	14.7	17.4	20.4	26.1 (22.1)
11. Japan (1880)	37.8	45.0	10.9	13.3	24.3	27.9		
12. United States (1971)	52.7	34.5	23.0	14.0	24.1	18.0	26.5	26.8 (28.8)
13. Canada	45.1	34.9	19.1	18.6	21.8	13.7	22.7	24.5 (24.3)

TABLE 4

Production and Trade of Twelve Leading Developed Countries, 1980

	Production[1]	Exports of Goods and Services		Exports of Goods	
	(Billions of $ U.S.)	(Billions of $ U.S.)	(Percent of GDP)	(Billions of $ U.S.)	(Percent GDP)
United States	2,587.1	260.8	10.0	216.7	8.4
Japan	1,040.0	145.1	14.0	129.2	12.4
West Germany	819.1	225.1	27.5	192.9	23.6
France	651.9	146.1	22.4	111.3	17.1
United Kingdom	522.9	148.5	28.4	115.1	22.0
Italy	394.0	99.5	25.2	77.7	19.7
Canada	253.3	74.3	29.3	65.0	25.6
Spain	211.1	32.9	15.6	20.7	9.8
Netherlands	167.6	89.0	53.1	74.0	44.1
Australia	140.0	25.4	181.1	22.0	15.7
Belgium Luxembourg	121.1	77.0	63.8	64.6	53.4

TABLE 5

Ratio of Merchandise Exports to Gross Domestic Product

	1965	1970	1973	1974	1975	1979	1980
United States	3.9	4.4	5.5	7.0	6.9	7.5	8.4
Japan	9.5	9.8	9.0	12.2	11.2	10.3	12.4
West Germany	15.6	18.4	19.6	23.4	21.4	22.6	23.6
France	10.2	12.5	14.3	17.1	15.4	17.1	17.1
United Kingdom	13.3	15.9	17.3	20.2	19.1	22.4	22.0
Canada	15.6	19.5	20.2	21.6	19.6	24.2	25.6
Italy	12.3	14.3	15.7	19.5	18.1	22.3	19.7
EECI (including intra-community trade)	15.2	18.1	20.0	23.8	21.3	23.4	23.6
EECI (excluding intra-community trade)	8.2	9.0	9.5	11.7	10.8	10.9	11.1
OECD	9.0	10.6	12.4	14.9	14.2	15.4	16.5

Source: Government of Canada, *A Review of Canadian Trade Policy* (Ottawa, 1983), pp. 20 - 22.

TABLE 6

Index of Regional Concentration in Manufacturing by Region 1870 - 1910

	1870	1880	1890	1900	1910	Share of value in Canadian manufacturing 1870	Share of value in Canadian manufacturing 1910
Atlantic	0.77	0.67	0.71	0.62	0.58	15.0	7.6
Quebec	0.07	1.03	0.98	1.49	1.03	33.3	21.7
Ontario	1.11	1.16	1.18	1.20	1.45	51.7	51.1
Prairies	-	0.43	0.44	0.34	0.34		6.4
British Columbia	-	1.09	1.55	1.42	1.14		6.2
Canada	1.00	1.00	1.00	1.00	1.00	100.0	100.0

* This index is simply a location quotient, the ratio of manufacturing value added per capita in a region to that in the country as a whole.

TABLE 7

Index of Concentration of Manufacturing Industries, by Region, 1880-1969

	1880	1910	1915	1969
Atlantic	0.67	0.58	0.63	0.36
Quebec	1.03	1.03	1.04	0.98
Ontario	1.16	1.45	1.53	1.53
Prairies	0.46	0.34	0.32	0.40
Pacific	1.09	1.14	0.85	0.85
Canada	1.00	1.00	1.00	1.00

Source: H. Pinchin, *The Regional Impact of the Canadian Tariff* (Ottawa, 1979), pp. 5 105

TABLE 8

Natural Increase and Estimated net Migration by Decades for Canada's Provinces, 1921-1931, 1931-1941, 1941-1951 and 1951-1961

(in 1,000s)

Province	1921 - 1931a		1931 - 1941a		1941 - 1951a		1951 - 1961a	
	Nat Inc	Nat Mig	Nat Inc.	Net Mig.	Nat. Inc.	Net Mig.	Nat Inc	Net Mig
Newfoundland	-	-	-	-	-	-	111	-14
Prince Edward Island	8	-9	10	-2	16	-13	18	-11
Nova Scotia	51	-62	57	+8	104	-39	128	-35
New Brunswick	57	-37	59	-10	100	-41	119	-37
Quebec	496	+17	459	-1	736	-12	998	+205
Ontario	343	+154	278	+78	505	+305	953	+685
Manitoba	99	-9	78	-48	108	-62	150	-4
Saskatchewan	153	+11	132	-158	135	-199	172	-79
Alberta	105	+40	106	-42	150	-7	265	+128
British Columbia	48	+121	41	+83	116	+231	224	+240
Yukon and Northwest Territories	-	-	1	+3	3	+4	9	+3

Source: W. Kalback and W.W. McVey, The Demographic Basis of Canadian Society (Toronto, 1971), p. 86.

TABLE 9

Degree of Industrialization and Finished manufacturers as a Proportion of Trade: 1913, 1929, 1955, and 1980 (per cent of total Trade)

	Exports				Imports
	1913	1929	1955	1980	1980
Industrial Countries					
Japan	31	43	64	71	11
Italy	31	41	47	61	28
Germany (Federal)	46	54	65	60	34
Sweden	23	26	33	53	45
United States	21	37	48	52	38
Great Britain	58	49	62	50	39
France	44	47	38	50	35
Canada	5	14	11	32	59
Semi-industrial Countries					
India	13	19	31.0	23	27
Brazil	-	-	0.4	22	29
Argentina	-	-	0.4	14	49
Australia	-	-	6.0	10	54
Turkey	-	-	0.4	7	39
Non-industrial Countries					
Egypt	-	-	3.0	4.0	35
Zaire	-	-	0.8	0.6	48
Burma	-	-	0.4	0.3	55

Source: G. Williams, *Not For Export*, p. 8.

7

HANDICRAFTS IN THE INDIAN ECONOMY: A STUDY OF THE HANDLOOM INDUSTRY FROM 1800*

J. Krishnamurty

In this paper we first examine broad trends in India's premier handicraft, the cotton handloom industry, considering loomage, employment and output for the periods 1800-1900 and 1900-1940. This is followed by an examination of regional contrasts in the pace and timing of decline (and recovery) over the whole period. Finally some general issues relating to research on handlooms are highlighted: the impact of progressive market integration in the subcontinent, the role of tastes and preferences and of comparative advantage in coarse and highly superior cloth in limiting the decline in handloom; the effects of technological and organizational changes; and, finally, the effect of all these factors on the weaver.

I

Information on the number of handlooms is not available on a systematic basis for the 19th century. For Madras Presidency, however, estimates exist for the period 1856-57 to 1860-61, when the number was placed at 2 lakhs. This could be an understatement as weavers probably understated looms to avoid the heavy burden of the motarfa tax.[1] The Board of Revenue suggested a figure of 2.25 lakhs. In 1921, only 169,425 looms were reported in the Presidency.[2] This would suggest that the industry was declining over the

*The results presented in this paper are tentative as they relate to research in progress. The author acknowledges his debt to Dr. K. Sundaram for his valuable suggestions.

1850-1920 period. But we cannot assume that output declined correspondingly, for as we shall see, considerably technological change occurred.

For India as a whole estimates of looms exist for the 20th century only. Around 1946-1951, there were about 2.3 million looms working on cotton textiles in India and Pakistan.[3] In 1940, of about 2 million looms in undivided India, 13 per cent were inactive and only 72 per cent of the remainder worked on cotton only. So about 1.26 million looms were actually working to produce cotton handloom products. The 1901 Census gave a figure of 2.7 million and the 1921 Census a figure of 2.0 million looms, but probably about 0.5 million looms were in Burma. So about 1.5 to 2.0 million looms were located in undivided India, compared to the 2 million reported in 1940 and about 2.3 million reported in 1946-51. But before drawing the conclusion that the industry expanded over the period, we need to remember that we have no estimate of active cotton handlooms for 1901-1921 and that 13 per cent of looms were inactive in 1940 and about 20 per cent were inactive in 1951 (Indian Union). So even for the first half of the 20th century, the data on looms is not unambiguous and the conclusions one can get would depend very much on the assumptions one makes.

In the absence of technological change one might regard looms as a proxy for output, but for the post 1900 period this is not valid. In 1940, it was reported that 35 per cent of all looms were of the improved variety (i.e., fly shuttle, not throw shuttle). The proportion would be about 40 per cent if we assume that the inactive looms were all of the throw shuttle variety. Again the reported proportion of fly shuttle looms to all looms was as high as 89 per cent in Travancore, 81 per cent in Madras and 78 per cent in Mysore; it was also quite high in Bengal (67 per cent) and Bombay (55 per cent).[4] Since the fly shuttle spread mainly after 1900 and since it had a much greater output capacity per period of time, the total number of looms and trends thereof do not adequately reflect the process of capacity creation, not to speak of utilization. For example it is claimed that in 1921, only about 8.5 per cent of looms were in the Madras Presidency yet about a quarter of the yarn consumed by the handloom sector is accounted for by this Presidency.[5]

It should be clear then that looking at the number of looms does not help very much in finding out what happened to the industry. Also, attempts to estimate employment from the number of looms involve further hazards. In some of the official reports of the 1940s and early 1950s it is assumed that 1 loom employs 2.5 workers, but the practice is not uniform and its empirical basis is difficult to establish. The norm would vary depending on many things including the quality and variety of the cloth.

Estimates of workers employed in handlooms typically include full-time and part-time workers. The Fact-finding Committee (Handloom and Mills), 1940[6] reported 1.434 million full-time weavers, 0.748 million paid assistants and 2.574 million unpaid assistants. There can be little doubt that their total of 4.7 million is inflated. To have a precise figure we would have to estimate it in full-time job equivalents, taking account of the duration of work during the year of the different types of workers.

The Textile Committee[7] estimated employment in handlooms to be 1.5 million for the Indian Union in 1954, and the Fact-finding Committee on Handlooms[8] estimated it to be 0.4 million in Pakistan in 1956. One may conclude that in the early fifties about 2 million were employed in handlooms. An alternative estimate based on Census data gives a figure of 1.8 million for the Indian Union in 1951.[9]

For the period 1911-1951, the employment in small-scale weaving appears to have declined from 1.93 to 1.80 million.[10] However, estimates based on Census data ignore part-time work; they record the responses of workers on the basis of their usual activity.

In an earlier work, Morris had argued that 4.7 million people were working in handlooms in the early 1950s.[11] This was perhaps based on the estimate of the Fact-finding Committee of 1942. But as it has been noted, the estimate is highly inflated and estimates for the early 1950s suggest a figure of about 2 million. Morris argues that if 4.7 million worked in handlooms in the 1950s, the absolute employment in this sector could not have declined between 1800 and 1950. According to Morris, if we assume that in 1800 the population of undivided India was 200 million and the work force 60 million, then an assumed 5 million workers in handlooms in 1800 would imply that this sector formed 8 per cent of the work force–a proportion which he regards to be far too high to be plausible. But our estimate of 2 million (instead of 4.7 million) for c. 1951 changes the story. On the same assumptions, only 4 per cent would be employed in handlooms. This is not at all implausible for the share of manufacturing in 1800 would lie in the region of 10-20 per cent of the work force.[12] Further, we can consider a variant in which the employment in handlooms declined from 3 million to 2 million over 1800-1951. This implies a 5 per cent share of handlooms in the 1800 work force–again, a not implausible level.

Twomey has recently attempted to estimate employment in handicraft cotton textiles using norms for converting yardage into full-time job equivalents (FTJE). His estimates suggest a decline in weaving from 1.8 million FTJE in 1800 to 1 million in 1880 and then a rise to 1.5 million in 1913 and to 1.7 million in 1929.[13] His assumptions of 3.5 FTJE per thousand yards cloth (including spinning) and 1.0 FTJE per thousand yards of cloth (weaving only) are based on evidence for 1940. In c. 1800, when machine yarn was absent, the FTJE per thousand yards may well have been higher. So the initial level of FTJEs (in 1800) in weaving may be higher than 1.8 million. In addition, the 1800 estimate of cloth output is conjectural: Twomey assumes that 190 million people[14] consume 9 yards per head–the letter assumption if virtually impossible to verify. Again Twomey's assumption that only 3 per cent of India's cloth output was being exported in the 1790s is implausible. This depends on Robson's estimate of Indian cloth exports which he placed at 50 million yards,[15] and on Twomey's own assumption of Indian cloth consumption of 1710 million yards around 1800. While Robson estimates imports into U.K. of calicoes and muslins to average 22 million yards during 1791-1800; another 10-15 million yards per annum going to Europe and America and some amount to Arabia and the Persian Gulf, his total of 50 million yards is very probably an underestimate since exports to the rest of Asia (an unknown magnitude) are assumed away.

So while Twomey's estimates do suggest a decline in weaving employment, many assumptions are built into it which are difficult to verify and which could affect the conclusion in many ways.

The evidence on employment in handlooms is consistent with a scenario of decline since 1800 in its absolute level and relative share in the work force. The available evidence would suggest that this decline was sharp in the 19th century, but had slowed down in the 20th century. The precise picture would have to be built up by looking at different parts of India and determining the magnitude, pace and timing of this decline.

Finally, we turn to the output estimates for handlooms. For the 1890s and thereafter, output has been calculated by estimating the yarn available to the handloom sector after taking into account imports and mill output of yarn not going into mill cloth. These estimates depend very much on the yarn-cloth conversion ratios assumed for handlooms and the mill sector (and changes in them over time) and are probably underestimates of levels since handspun yarn is not taken into account. On the same ground, assuming that handspun yarn output in the 1890s was significant and declined thereafter, they may overstate the growth rate of handloom output (inclusive of *khadi*).

Bell provides estimates using the method described in the preceding paragraph, for the period 1896-97 to 1900-01 (Table 1).

TABLE 1

Cloth Output (Supply) in India, 1896-97 to 1900-01

		Million Yards (annual average)
1.	Foreign Cloth (net of imports)	1,932
2.	Indian Mill Cloth (including exports)	404
3.	Handloom (including exports)	846

Source: R.D. Bell, *Notes on the Indian Textiles Industry with Special Reference to Handweaving*, Bulletin No. 6, Department of Industries, Bombay Presidency, Bombay, 1926, Table V and VI, pp. 16-17.

The estimates for handloom cloth in 1900 do not take account of cloth produced with handspun yarn. Using estimates of cotton output Twomey calculates that in 1895-99, about 480 million yards of this cloth (*khadi*) was produced annually.[16] This is probably an overestimate since cotton output is generally overestimated in this period duc to unduly high normal fields being used. But using this estimate, total cloth consumption around 1900 would be 3559 million yards and handloom's share would be 1326 million yards.

We next construct our scenario in which handloom output (consumption) is set at 1326 million yards for 1800 as well and the population is taken to be 179 million in 1800 and 285 million 1900.[17] In 1800 handlooms are the sole source of cloth supply. This scenario implies that cloth consumption rose from 1326 to 3559 million yards per annum over the century and per head consumption from 7.4 to 12.5 yards over the period. This implies an increase of 168 per cent aggregate cloth consumption and of 69 per cent in per head consumption over the century.

Our scenario does not take account of handloom exports in 1800, which as we have noted earlier, were certainly higher than 50 million yards. Larger the export volume, lower will be domestic aggregate and per head availability of cloth in 1800 and greater will be the corresponding increase for the century as a whole. Hence the large increases reported here could be underestimates of the consumption implications of a scenario in which no decline in handloom output over the century is permitted.

Such large increase in aggregate consumption and per head consumption of cloth over the century appear implausible. Much more information is needed about changes in clothing patterns over the period. While one might stress the increased use of Saris and blouses, one could equally claim that turbans were on the decline: in effect, for each social class and for the two sexes, changes in the demand for cloth would have to be assessed for each region and aggregated for India as a whole. Unfortunately the social history of dress in 19th century India is still in its infancy; the evidence is patchy and conclusions are unclear.

An alternative way of assessing the scenario would be to use estimates of price and income elasticities of demand. These are available for 1880-1930 for cloth consumption in Twomey's paper.[18] The price elasticity of aggregate cloth consumption turns out to be very low, -0.30. This means that price declines over the century could not have increased cloth consumption by even 30 per cent. The income elasticity is +0.80 which is fairly high. Since aggregate cloth consumption increased by 168 per cent over the century, aggregate real income must have more than tripled if the price and income effects are to result in such a large increase in aggregate cloth consumption. Given that population grew by 59 per cent over the period, this order of required increase in aggregate income would, in turn, imply a very sharp rise in per capita income which may be safety ruled out. This suggests that aggregate cloth consumption must have increased much less rapidly and this immediately sustains the conclusion that handloom cloth output in 1800 was much larger than the level assumed in the scenario. The implication then is that handloom cloth output declined over the century.

The purpose of the scenario is to show that handloom output almost certainly declined in absolute terms between 1800 and 1900. For the period after 1900 we do have estimates which suggest that handloom output rose from 965 million yards in 1902-03/1912-13 to not less than 1068 million yards in 1930-31/1937-38. Of course, this ignores what happened to *khadi*, on which there is little reliable evidence.[19]

Taking the period 1800-1940, one can then assert that there was a sharp decline in handloom output up to about 1900 and some recovery thereafter. But if the broad magnitudes given have some basis, it is clear that the twentieth century saw some recovery, but most probably not to the levels obtaining in the early nineteenth century.

This conclusion is at variance with that of Morris in his most recent analysis where he claims: "Allowing for the rise in demand that was associated with population growth and price elasticity, it is hard to believe that absolute output of handloom declined much if at all."[20]

II

We have so far looked at the fate of handloom textiles over the period 1800-1940, concentrating on broad trends at the all-India level. However, the really interesting issues relate to what happened within these broad all-India trends. The author has shown in his study elsewhere that in the 19th century the industry certainly underwent a decline in Gangetic Bihar and probably the same was true of Bengal proper.[21] Evidence of partial recovery in the 20th century has been presented in the present paper. However, the regional contrasts need to be elaborated further.

Regarding the 19th century, Gadgil has argued that the decline of handicrafts was not universal for "the periods different from one part of the country to another, for though Bengal was affected by foreign competition in the earlier part of the nineteenth century the Central Provinces industry was not touched till after the sixties."[22] The decline of handicrafts (including textiles) occurred in Rajasthan only after 1911 when the region was "opened up" by the railways.[23] Rajat Ray has recently argued that in the Ahmedabad region the 19th century may have seen some expansion in handloom output as mill yarn replaced hand-spun yarn.[24] In the Deccan the evidence points to a large decline as Manchester textiles flooded the market which was readily accessible via Bombay. As early as 1832, imports appear to have hit domestic weaving. Sykes informed the Select Committee (1832) that there were hardly any manufactures left in the Deccan; they were reduced to the production of coarse cotton cloth and blankets.[25] Even earlier in 1830, Elphinstone and Chaplin had noted the decline in domestic weaving, in their evidence before the Select Committee (1830).[26] At the end of the century, Enthoven in the official monograph on textiles reluctantly admits: ". . . the effects of the competition from English-made goods has already been fully experienced, the imported fabrics having forced the handloom industry to fall back on its present class of manufactures before the expansion of the local power industry commenced to take effect."[27] In a specific study of handicrafts in the Deccan, Joshi shows how the development of the railways integrated the market and led to a decline in handloom in most lines except women's wear and coarse cloth where consumer preference and competitive power favored the handloom.[28]

In South India too, imports appear to have hit handlooms hard. According to Thurston,[29] "the bazaars of Southern India are flooded with imported piece goods of British manufacture. . . . The exports have shrunk into trifling insignificance, while the import of piece goods (cotton and linen) to the ports of Madras have . . . assumed vast proportions." In respect of specific and important centres like Madura, Kumbakonam, Conjeeveram and Venkatagiri, the evidence is of decline; though handlooms survive, they are pushed into the production of coarse cloth.

During the 20th century while Rajasthan's handloom industry was hit by the spread of railways exposing it to outside competition, in many parts of India the industry made a recovery. This generally involved the adoption of improved looms which helped to improve the competitive power of the industry, but organizationally too there were changes: progressively the weaver was coming under the grip of merchant-middlemen and *karkhana* owners and his earnings, often wages, were probably declining.

In the Madras Presidency, the early 20th century saw a major technological breakthrough with the spread of the fly-shuttle. Chatterton, the pioneer of the new loom, shows that the output effects must have been quite considerable. According to him: ". . . it has been worked out very carefully as to what the advantages are in substituting the ordinary fly-shuttle for the indigenous slay . . . and the average comes to Rs. 2/8 (Rs. 2.50 a month). In the south of India over 100,000 of these slays have been put in. . . . These 100,000 looms have enabled the weaver to earn another 2.5 lakhs a month".[30] As we have noted earlier, by 1940 eighty-one per cent of looms in Madras Presidency were of the fly-shuttle variety. The output effect of the new technology may be judged from the fact that while the Presidency accounted in 1931 for only 8.5 per cent of all-India looms, it consumed about a quarter of the yarn available for handloom weaving all over India.[31] However the condition of weavers in Madras appears to have deteriorated between 1928 and 1941. According to the Fact-finding Committee, monthly earnings in 13 centres in the Presidency declined by 50 per cent or more. They attribute this to the growth of merchant and *Sowcar* control and the development of the *karkhana* system.[32]

In Bombay also, the position of handlooms appears to have improved in the first half of the century. About 55 per cent of looms were of the fly-shuttle variety by 1940. Joshi's assessment is that up to the early 1930s, a number of factors helped to keep up demand for handlooms.[33] The first World War hit imports of cloth and machinery and thereby helped handlooms. Again Swadeshi sentiments in the 1920s may have helped as also labor troubles in the Bombay mills. Joshi feels that during the 1900-1930 period, handloom production expanded in the Deccan. As in Madras, the growth of *karkhanas* and of indebtedness among weavers went along with declining monthly earnings of weavers which fell again by 50 per cent or more between 1928 and 1941 in the 8 centers for which estimates are reported by the Fact-finding Committee. An interesting picture of the handloom weaver of Bombay is provided in the official monograph of 1909. According to Mehta, the author, handloom weavers fell into four categories. About 5 per cent were sowcar-weavers, buying raw materials in quantity and stocking finished goods, using family and hired labor and lending yarn to others and buying cloth from others. About a quarter, bought yarn and wove it themselves. These were viable in good years but in bad times did have to sell at a loss and borrow yarn from others. About one half were indebted to weaver-sowcar, had pledged their looms and worked for the weaver-sowcar to pay off the debt. The remaining 20 odd per cent were hopelessly indebted and often houseless. These weavers were totally at the mercy of the sowcar.[34]

For Bengal proper, I have not as yet examined the evidence. But we do know that in 1940, about 67 per cent of the looms were of the fly-shuttle variety and that wages between 1928 and 1941 fell by 50 per cent or more in the 5 centres for which data was obtained.[35] Unlike Bombay and Madras, the *karkhana* system does not appear to have made much headway.[36] Some revival in handlooms is reported by Cummings for the Bengal Presidency in 1908. According to him the Swadeshi movement in 1906 and 1907 was "a new factor stimulating production and creating demand. I find that this has led to the improvement of the weaver in parts of the Presidency and Burdwan Division; that is to say, many weavers who had given up their caste occupation have returned to it."[37]

For Bihar and Orissa again 20th century developments are unclear and the evidence that is available for U.P. would suggest that the industry continued to decline.[38]

III

The limited information presented above suggests that in many parts of India there was a revival in handlooms, though this was not uniform over space.[39] In mainland north India, the decline probably continued as new areas were integrated into the national market by the expansion of the railways. The pace, pattern and timing of changes in this sector in different parts of India is still to be adequately mapped. It should also be clear that the output declines of the 19th century and even the progress made in the 20th century were associated with complex processes whereby weavers lost some of their traditional rights and their place in the community, faced lower living standards and greater indebtedness. The shift from hand to machine yarn, from the household to the *karkhana*, from local to more distant and often more uncertain markets had serious consequences on the quality of life of the weaver. In the long run these changes occurred alongside a secular decline in the market for handlooms, for 20th century expansion could not outweigh the massive declines that occurred in the 19th century.

At the same time, we can no longer assume that the early 19th century was the best of all possible worlds for the weaver. Even in that period many weavers depended at least partially on agriculture, many were seriously in debt and often they did not enjoy a high status in the local community.[40]

To conclude, Indian handlooms declined sharply in the face of competition from Manchester and later from the Indian mills. To some extent there was a recovery after 1900 in which technological progress in the form of the fly-shuttle had a major role. The pace of the process of decline and its spread across India depended on a number of factors. First, the most accessible areas felt the impact the earliest, and slowly the impact percolated into the interior as transport developed and markets became more integrated. Secondly, handlooms survived partly by concentrating on non-competitive products like coarse country cloth at one end and very superior, luxury products at the other. In some areas (e.g., Bombay) the demand for women's garments remained with handloom, while in some other areas (e.g., Madras), the move to Manchester coloured prints was widespread among both sexes. In general consumer tastes and preferences, and changes in them over time were important determinants of the fate of handlooms. Thirdly, the fly-shuttle after 1920 probably made handlooms competitive on a wider range of products. We need comparable prices of mill (domestic and imported) and handloom cloth over time to see to what extent relative costs were moving again in favour of handlooms. Finally, while the condition of the weavers declined over time, it should be remembered that they were probably not good to start with.

NOTES

1. D. Kumar (ed.). *The Cambridge Economic History of India*, Vol. II, Chapter III, 4, p. 369. This tax, which was a tax on professions and trades, was abolished in Bengal in 1793 and in Bombay in 1844.
2. *Census of India, 1931*, Madras. Part I, Report, by M.W.M. Yeatts, Calcutta, 1932, pp. 226-227.
3. Government of India, *Report of the Textile Enquiry Committee*, 1954, Delhi, 1954. Pakistan; Ministry of Industries, *Report of the Fact-finding Committee on Handlooms*, Karachi, 1956, p. 12.
4. India, *Report of the Fact-Finding Committee (Handloom and Mills)*, 1940.
5. *Census of India 1931*, Madras, Part I, Report, by Calcutta 1932, pp. 226-227.
6. Government of India. *Report of the Fact-finding Committee (Handloom and Mills)*, Calcutta, 1942, pp. 35-36.
7. Government of India, *Report of the Textile Enquiry Committee*, 1954, Delhi, 1954, Vol. I, pp. 16-17.
8. Government of Pakistan. Ministry of Industries, *Report of the Fact-finding Committee on Handlooms*. Karachi, 1956, p. 21.
9. J. Krishnamurty, "The Distribution of the Indian Working Force, 1901-1951," in K.N. Chaudhuri and C.J. Dewey (ed.), *Economy and Society: Essays in Indian Economic and Social History*, Delhi, 1979, pp. 273.

10. *Ibid.*, Table 6. The details of the calculations are also provided therein.
11. M.D. Morris *et.al., The Indian Economy in the Nineteenth Century: A Symposium*, Delhi, 1969, pp. 159-165.
12. In the 20th century, it was around 10 per cent and Bagchi's estimates for Gangetic Bihar for 1809-13 give a figure of about 18 per cent of the population dependent on manufacturing.
13. Michael J. Twomey, "Employment in Nineteenth Century Indian Textiles," *Exploration in Economic History*, Vol. 20, 1983, p. 37-57.
14. Twomey also has a "Low" estimate of 110 million which I have disregarded. See Twomey, *op. cit.*, p. 54.
15. R. Robson, *The Cotton Industry in Britain*, London, 1957, p. 1, especially footnote.
16. Twomey, "Employment in Nineteenth Century Indian Textiles," p. 46.
17. The 1800 population is by Sen Gupta *et. al.*, reported in D. Kumar (ed.), *Cambridge Economic History of India*, Vol. II, Table 5.1
18. Twomey, "Employment in Nineteenth Century Indian Textiles," Table 7, equation 5.
19. While we do not go into the fate of hand spinning, it is clear that this activity did not disappear after 1800, though it declined sharply. The poor in some parts of India did use a coarse cloth (*Motia or Gazi*) which was often hand-spun. See N.N. Banerji, *Monograph on the Cotton Fabrics of Bengal*, Calcutta, 1898, p. 32.
20. D. Kumar (ed.), *Cambridge Economic History of India*, Vol. II, p. 671. A conclusion similar to mine is reached by Bagchi for the 1900-1939 period. See A.K. Bagchi, *Private Investment in India 1900-1939*, Cambridge, 1972, pp. 219-228.
21. J. Krishnamurty, "Deindustrialisation in Gangetic Bihar: A Case Study of the Cotton Textile Industry, 1809-1898," DSE Working Paper 241, March 1983 (mimeo).
22. D.R. Gadgil, *The Industrial Evolution of India in Recent Times* 1860-1939: Delhi, 1971, esp. pp. 178-179.
23. See D. Kumar (ed.), *Cambridge Economic History of India*; Vol. II, 1983, p. 546.
24. Rajat Ray, "Pedhis and Mills: The Historical Integration of the Formal and Informal Sectors in the Economy of Ahmedabad," *Indian Economic and Social History Review*, Vol. XIV Nos. 3-4, July-December 1982, espl. pp. 390-391.
25. See R.D. Choksey, *Economic History of the Bombay Deccan and Karnatak* (1818-1868), Poona, 1945, pp. 213-215.
26. *Ibid.*, p. 212.
27. R.E. Enthoven, *Monograph on Cotton Fabrics in Bombay Presidency*, Bombay, 1897, p. 35. Enthoven's remarks relate to the Presidency as a whole, not to Deccan alone.
28. N.M. Joshi, *Urban Handicrafts of the Bombay Deccan*, Poona, 1936, pp. 48-49.
29. Edgar Thurston, *Monograph on the Cotton Fabric Industry of the Madras Presidency* (1901), (reprinted in *Arts and Industry through the Ages)*, New Delhi, p. 27.
30. Government of India, *Report of the India Industrial Commission, Minutes of Evidence, 1916-17*, Bombay; Calcutta, 1917, p. 57.
31. *Census of India 1931*, Madras, Part I, Report by M. W.M. Yeats, Calcutta, 1932, pp. 226-7.
32. Government of India, *Report of the Fact-finding Committee (Handloom and Mills)*, Calcutta, 1942, pp. 199-200 and p. 70.

33. N.M. Joshi, *Urban Handicrafts of the Bombay Deccan*, Poona, 1936, pp. 90-91.
34. P.N. Mehta, *Report on the Handloom Industry*, Bombay, 1909 (Bombay Government Publication), espl. p. 1.
35. Government of India, *Report of the Fact-finding Committee (Handloom and Mills)*, Calcutta, 1942, pp. 199-200.
36. *Ibid.*, p. 70.
37. Bengal, Industrial Enquiries, J.G. Cummings, *Review of the Industrial Position and Prospects in Bengal 1908 with Special Reference to the Industrial Survey of 1890*, Calcutta, 1908, p. 6.
38. Unpublished data on U.P. from Rubab Azad's forthcoming M.Phil dissertation (Delhi University) would suggest that hand textiles declined sharply in terms of employment even after 1900. Also see Gyan Pandey "Economic Dislocation in Nineteenth Century Eastern U.P.: Some Implications of the Decline of Artisanal Industry in Colonial India," Centre for Studies in Social Sciences, Calcutta, Occasional Paper 37. This however relates to the 19th century.
39. For somewhat similar conclusions and a useful discussion see A.K. Bagchi: *Private Investment in India, 1900-1939*, Cambridge, 1972, pp. 219-228.
40. For a discussion of this aspect see J. Krishnamurty, "Deindustrialisation in Gangetic Bihar: A Case Study of the Cotton Textile Industry," DSE Working Paper No. 241, March 1983, (mimeo), pp. 11-12.